W9-DGS-713

This Book
was purchased
with funds
provided by the
DeKalb County
Farm Bureau

© 1987 GAYLORD

CROSSING THE COLOR LINE

Crossing the Color Line

RACE, PARENTING, AND CULTURE

Maureen T. Reddy

RUTGERS UNIVERSITY PRESS
New Brunswick, New Jersey

Library of Congress Cataloging-in-Publication Data

Reddy, Maureen T.
Crossing the color line : race, parenting, and culture / by
Maureen T. Reddy.
p.   cm.
Includes bibliographical references and index.
ISBN 0-8135-2105-X
1. Children of interracial marriage—United States—Case studies.
2. Parent and child—United States. 3. Racism—United States.
I. Title.
HQ777.9.R43   1994
305.8—dc20   94-535
                                                       CIP

British Cataloging-in-Publication information available

For Doug, with love

Contents

Preface

Imagine:

Your nine-year-old son likes to play hide-and-seek games around the neighborhood with other children. One afternoon, you look out the kitchen window and see him crouching behind a neighbor's hedge, with his dark jacket pulled up over the back of his head for camouflage. Suddenly realizing that your child is now tall enough to be mistaken for a teenager, you call him into the house, away from the game. He thinks his greatest danger is being found by the child who is "It," but you know that he is at risk of being shot by someone who sees not a child playing, but the urban predator of television-fueled nightmares, ready to spring from the bushes.

You know that you have waited too long to warn him about this danger, and about others that are real and present now that he resembles an adolescent. He has to be told to keep his hands out of his pockets when he is in stores, for instance, lest he be seen as a shoplifter. He also must learn how to talk to the police who will surely stop him when he is out riding his bike some day soon. You ask your son to feed his pets and to make his bed, hoping the chores will give you enough time to figure out how to explain these facts of life to him without destroying his innocent sense of fun. You never faced such dangers as a child, and so you have no model to follow.

Unless you are white and your family is black, you probably will never confront exactly the dilemma I did early in 1992.[1] If everyone in your family is white, you would not have to teach your child to protect himself from these particular dangers. If you are black, you would have familial and personal experience to draw upon in teaching your children how to negotiate the world safely, with their self-esteem and sense of possibility protected. A white person in a black family starts from scratch.

Many Americans of all races want to believe that raising children is basically the same project, regardless of the children's and parents' races, arguing that child-rearing issues lack racial inflections.[2] And some aspects of parenting are indeed race-blind: toilet training, for example, or treating common childhood illnesses. However, I have learned as a white mother of black children that the race-blind issues tend to be the easier issues, and that far more of the hard questions I have about raising my children center on race. This should not be a surprise in a society as racialized as the one in which we live. Pick up a newspaper in any urban area in the United States on any day, and it is virtually certain that you will find at least one major story on race, with none of the news good: charges of racial discrimination in hiring practices, debates about affirmative action, high unemployment among so-called minority groups, racial violence, racial tensions—all these are front-page staples. The grim statistics on black life chances are familiar, at least in outline. Whereas blacks make up 12.1 percent of the U.S. population, they earn only 7.2 percent of the aggregate family income, and receive only 5.7 percent of all bachelor's degrees and 3.5 percent of doctorates awarded by U.S. colleges and universities.[3] Blacks are overrepresented in prisons (45.3% of inmates), as victims of crime (50.8 percent of murder victims, 33.2 percent of rape victims, and 30.8 percent of robbery victims were black in 1989–90), and in ill-paid occupations (25 percent of hotel maids are black, for example, but only 0.9 percent of architects are).[4] In 1990, blacks were nearly three times as likely to be unemployed as were whites and nearly four times as likely to live in poverty, earning only approximately $580 for each $1,000 earned by white families.[5] Blacks have a far higher infant mortality rate than do whites, and if they live past infancy they are more likely to die young of hypertension, diabetes, or AIDS than are whites. The terrible facts that young black men are more than twice as likely to be homicide victims than they are to attend college and that murder is the leading cause of death for young black men are old news.

For the most part, even well-intentioned whites have no clear idea of the daily lives of their black fellow citizens, of what it feels like to live with racism every day. Worse yet, what it feels like to look at one's beloved children and to realize that the limited life chances limned by statistics are *their* life chances. Every so often, American whites are forced by some especially troubling public event to consider what such statistics might really mean to blacks, to confront at least briefly the flesh-and-blood reality of racism in America. The 1992 Los Angeles uprising might seem such an event, as it briefly focused attention on the "underclass," which was depicted as black by the media. In fact, though, the participants in the uprising were *not* all black; the media's persistence in protraying it as a black riot missed the point and misrepresented the case while reinforcing stereotypes about race.[6] To my mind, one of the most powerful recent statements on the insidious extent of racism in our time came from Arthur Ashe in 1992. Frail, dying of AIDS, but as calm as ever, Ashe told an interviewer that having AIDS was not the most difficult thing he had ever had to deal with—being black was. Ashe's money and fame did not protect him from racism, as indeed nothing could.

And yet, the story on race is not all grim. Racism affects all black people, but racism is not the sum of black people's lives. Further, racism is subject to change, can even be eradicated through the collective efforts of blacks and whites working together. First, however, we as a nation need a serious, sustained, meaningful dialogue about race. As Cornel West points out, most Americans "remain trapped in the narrow framework of the dominant liberal and conservative views of race in America," neither of which recognize black people and their experiences as *"constitutive elements of* [American] *life."*[7] This book documents my own journey toward an internalized understanding of race— white and black—and racism as the white wife of a black husband and the white mother of black children, challenging along the way both white views of blacks and black views of whites. My hope is that *Crossing the Color Line* will contribute to that necessary, long-delayed national engagement with race.

This book includes literary analysis, but it is not a book of literary analysis. It includes stories from my life, but it is not strictly an autobiography. It uses material from interviews, but it is not social research. It draws on theory and develops theory, but it is not a theoretical text, either. My main models in writing this book are works by black feminist theorists: bell hooks's *Talking Back: Thinking Feminist, Thinking Black*, Patricia Hill Collins's *Black Feminist Thought*, and Patricia Williams's *The Alchemy of Race and Rights*, all texts that cross genre boundaries. These three writers draw on their daily experiences and their personal and familial histories to illuminate social and theoretical issues, and vice versa. Like hooks, Collins, and Williams, I believe theory has "everyday" roots that must be made visible and that it must have "everyday" uses to be worth doing. One of these everyday uses is to place my children's and my own personal experiences in a cultural context that we, and other interracial families, can use. Another is to create a theoretical framework that can acccount for some of the implications of color-line crossing and that might therefore contribute to race theory and to racial liberation.

Although I often quote my husband in this book, *Crossing the Color Line* is not about us or about him, but about me, particularly my experiences as a white feminist mother of black children and the links between that experience and developing theories of race and gender. Because I want to focus on some of these larger theoretical issues, I have chosen to tell my story achronologically for the most part, clustering personal experiences together on the basis of shared themes. The first chapter, "On Lines and Bridges," explores my beginning to come to terms with my ambiguous racial position. My second chapter, "Starting Out," sketches Doug's and my early relationship, before the birth of Sean in 1983. The third chapter, "Why Do White People Have Vaginas?," examines the impact of Sean's developing awareness of racial categories and gender roles on my thinking about race and gender. The fourth, " 'One Drop of Black Blood,' " juxtaposes literary, theoretical, and personal accounts of awakening racial identities. The fifth chapter, "The Fourth R," looks at how schools teach racism, using Sean's experience as the grounding narrative. The last chapter, "Mothers, Daughters, Sisters, Comrades," considers relationships between black and white women, particularly in the framework of the contemporary women's movement, with my daughter Ailis's birth in 1991 a crucial element of concern.

Although I speak about African-American lives in this book, I am not an "authority" on African-American people; I am a student, gaining insight from the work of African-American scholars, especially black women theoreticians. Nor am I—or anyone—an authority on motherhood in general. I am, however, an authority on my own experience, and I try throughout *Crossing the Color Line* to speak from that experience and particularly from the position of an ally in the struggle for black liberation.

Black people's voices are heard throughout this book, but in an important way *Crossing the Color Line* is not *about* black people, although it is about race: it is about whiteness, about trying to cross the color line at many places, about the meeting

Acknowledgments

A great many people helped with *Crossing the Color Line*. I am especially indebted to the friends and relatives who have allowed me to write about our shared experiences and even sometimes to quote their words. To protect their privacy, I have used pseudonyms for everyone outside my family and for my children as well. At ten and two, my son and daughter are far too young to grant me anything like informed consent, and so I want to give them the protection of concealing their real names. My son is very disappointed that I have not used his actual name, but pleased that his name is the *only* part of his story that I have changed.

I am also deeply grateful to Jane Lazarre and Martha Roth, who generously read the penultimate draft of this book and offered enormously helpful suggestions. All writers have ideal readers, and as I was writing *Crossing the Color Line*, I realized that Jane and Martha are my ideal readers, that I had them always in mind as I wrote. Jane's life and work inspire me. Our many talks over the years about the multiple intersections of our lives have helped both to shape my identity as a white mother of black children and to give me the courage to write about that experience. Martha, a dear friend as well as a very sharp reader, inspires me with her commitment to both feminist politics and intellectual clarity. I have tried to follow Jane's and Martha's invaluable advice when revising.

Leslie Mitchner of Rutgers University Press saw the germ of a book in an essay of mine that she read, and encouraged me to write *Crossing the Color Line*. Without her vision, there would be no book, and without her gentle but firm guidance, this book would be far poorer. While I was working on this book, my daughter was born, and both my father and my father-in-law died. Leslie stuck with me through all of this emotional upheaval, and gave me confidence in this project. There are not words sufficient to express how grateful I am.

Rhode Island College gave the project a boost by providing released time from teaching, as well as research grants and funding for assistants. Two graduate students, Paula Delfiore and Ann Murphy, haunted the library for me and helped me to straighten out a very messy bibliography. Ann also did a preliminary draft of the index. I appreciate Ann's and Paula's work very much.

I want also to thank Willa Speiser for her excellent copy editing, and my son, husband, and sister for proofreading.

CROSSING THE COLOR LINE

1
On
Lines
and
Bridges

HALFWAY ACROSS the Tappan Zee Bridge, I am seized by a paralyzing terror as I involuntarily and vividly imagine the bridge splintering to pieces, sending cars tumbling into the Hudson. My heart races, the pounding of blood in my ears drowns out the radio, my foot on the gas pedal begins to go numb. I am sure that I'm going to faint and cause the car to career over the guardrail. Clutching the steering wheel with sweaty hands, I frantically look for a place to pull over, but repair crews have closed off several lanes and there is nowhere for me to stop.

My two-year-old son, strapped into his car seat in the back, must sense something amiss, as he stops singing to ask, "Is this Grandma's? We there?" "No, Sean, but we're almost there," I reply in a high-pitched, strangled-sounding voice. Speaking seems to lessen my terror, and so I continue, alternately talking loudly to Sean—"We're going to be at Grandma's in just a little while"—and mumbling quietly to myself, "You're not going to die, you're going to drive across this bridge, you've done it dozens of times, thousands of people do it every day, the bridge is safe, follow the car in front of you, don't look out the side, this is exactly like a highway, there's nothing to be afraid of, you're just having a panic attack." As I name it to myself, I grasp what is happening—yes, this must be a panic attack. Somehow, labeling the fear diminishes it a bit, and I am able to drive across the bridge without mishap. Once I pay the toll on the other side, I pull over to the shoulder to get a grip on myself. My knees are trembling uncontrollably, and the steering wheel is slippery wet. Sean pipes up, "This Grandma's house?"

Laughing with relief—we're okay, the Tappan Zee is behind us, the panic is over—I say, "Sean, honey, does this *look* like Grandma's house? Hang on, we're almost there," and pull back into the traffic, once more in control.

Ten minutes later, we are at my in-laws' house, meeting my husband, Doug, who has been in New York all week on business. Pulled into the warmth and talk of a family gathering, I feel safe and happy, *normal*. I briefly consider telling my husband or my mother-in-law about my inexplicable panic on the bridge, but don't want to worry anyone or to embarrass myself. In the end I keep quiet. Going home to Philadelphia on Sunday evening, Doug drives. The Tappan Zee doesn't bother me at all this time, and I decide the panic was a once-in-a-lifetime event.

As it turns out, I am wrong. During the next few months, whenever I must drive over a bridge, the same panic begins again. The fear strikes only when I am the driver, never when I am a passenger. I start planning my routes carefully, trying to avoid even highway overpasses, and then berate myself for giving in to this phobia. At thirty, having never been afraid of anything much—indeed, having sometimes frightened other people with my recklessness—I find my world shrinking to places I can get to without crossing bridges. I wonder, then, am I going crazy? My reluctance to tell anyone about this phobia soon hardens into a shamed secrecy. Finally, the inevitable moment arrives. Once again, we are going to New York; Doug is too tired to drive, and I am at the wheel as we approach the Tappan Zee. When the dreaded panic symptoms begin, I say abruptly to Doug, "Start talking. You have to talk me over this bridge, or else I'll have some sort of breakdown, faint or something." Thinking it's a joke, he laughs, but then looks searchingly at me and starts talking.

Later, I tell a still-astonished Doug the three-month history of my struggle with bridge terror. I can't determine which worries him more: my fear or my long silence, as both are completely out of character for me. Together, we agree that I should probably see a counselor about the bridge phobia, but— and this is *in* character—I procrastinate for years. However, once I've told Doug about the bridge panic, it seems possible to tell others, and I start talking to friends about it. Several people admit to similar fears—of bridges, tunnels, escalators, highways, airplanes, trains, you name it. I am amazed at the litany of terrors people confess to me. A colleague who teaches psychology gives me an article that says bridge phobia is very common, and is related to fear of heights. However, I am not afraid of heights and do not fit any of the profiles of typical bridge-phobics the article gives. Although talking about my fear has made me feel less crazy, I still have the fear five years later and am no closer to understanding its origin than I was that first day it struck on the Tappan Zee. For years, bridge phobia rides along with me whenever I drive, lessening across time but never really gone, always ready to spring, like some malevolent ghost in the back seat.

And then, during a conversation about interracial marriages, a friend remarks, "I don't think I would ever marry a white man; there'd be too much trouble with his family, I assume. But if I did, he'd know from the start that he'd have to assimilate into the black community, like you have." Startled by this description of my position and searching for the words that will explain how I see myself—a white woman married to a black man, a white mother of black children—I say, "I don't think a white person can really *assimilate*; the color line doesn't work that way. I'm still white. I think I stand on the color line itself, not on one side of it. Or maybe I'm like a bridge, stretching across the line, touching both sides, but mostly in the middle somewhere." As I say this, I have a visual image of my body as a bridge that strikes me with the force of an epiphany: *that's the* source of the bridge panic, I realize with a strange elation. The panic is not about heights or speed or water, but about metaphor and race.

It was not the Tappan Zee that was in danger of falling apart in 1985, but me. The onset of my bridge phobia coincided with Sean's searching first questions about race. Although I had not put these two facts together before the conversation about marrying across the color line, I understand now that they were causally related. Driving across that bridge literalized my metaphoric position, which was becoming more complicated and stressful than it ever had been before, and I panicked. Identifying the source of the panic also helped to explain why the phobia had waned so much in recent months, as I had finally become comfortable with my own racial position, in particular with the multiple, ever-evolving meanings of being the white mother of black children.[1]

Until Sean was two, Doug and I believed that race shed its public significance outside our apartment door. Doug does not look at me and see a white woman, but Maureen, his wife, just as I do not see him as a black man, but as Doug, my husband. Not so remarkable, really: I don't think most people habitually think of their lovers or children or parents in generic terms or as having a particular race or ethnicity—we know each other too well for that, and the issues with which we grapple are not about race but about time and housework and schedules and all of life's flotsam and jetsam. Contrary to what one might expect from the received wisdom, none of the very few problems Doug and I have had in our marriage have been caused by a racial gap between us. In fact, I think we have had fewer misunderstandings of any kind than do most couples, because from the beginning we knew that the external pressures on us would be enormous and that we would have to keep the inner strength to deal with them together. In other words, inside our marriage, racial differences have worked *for* us. We have both changed and grown over the years, in shapes and in directions that I partly attribute to this external pressure.

Sean, at two, was just learning about race; he was becoming "raced," and was "re-racing" Doug and me in unsettling ways. And yet, this is not quite accurate, either: we were *always* raced, just as we were always gendered, with our races central parts of our identities. All that I had ever thought and done, I had thought and done as a white female. All that Doug had ever thought and done, he had thought and done as a black male. Neither of us grew up in a bubble, isolated from our society, and of course every intimate detail of our lives had been shaped by that society. And yet we both knew and did not know the implications of these truths. Until Sean became aware of race, many of the byzantine subtleties of race were not articulated by either of us and remained just beneath consciousness much of the time—*there* in our lives always, but beyond our control and not about *us*. We usually talked about race in terms of public events rather than private meanings: we were both struggling for and committed to the same side of the color line, and that's what mattered. I did not feel like a bridge, stretching uncomfortably across that color line, until Sean awakened me from what in retrospect seems a delusion of colorlessness.

W R I T I N G   I N   1 9 0 3 ,   W . E . B .   D U B O I S asserted in *The Souls of Black Folk* that "the problem of the Twentieth Century is the problem of the color-line."[2] As this century draws to an end, it appears that the problem of the twenty-first century will also be the problem of the color line. DuBois saw the color line as dividing whites and blacks both publicly and privately, keeping most jobs, money, neighborhoods, educational opportunities, and political power on the white side of that line and consequently separating white and black consciousnesses. Black people, DuBois averred, live behind a veil that whites do not penetrate and that gives blacks a "double-consciousness." In *The Souls of Black Folk*, he proposed to lift that veil, to offer whites glimpses of black life and thought in hopes of destroying racial segregation. Despite DuBois's and many others' efforts, both veil and racial separation remain.

The bridge metaphor that had such force in my own life suggests that the distance between blacks and whites more closely resembles a chasm or a river than a mere line, and certainly the daily lives of blacks and whites in the United States diverge so greatly that it sometimes seems we inhabit different universes. Again and again, white and black people report widely differing experiences and attitudes. For example, in a 1992 Boston *Globe* study of black and white people aged eighteen to twenty-nine—the post–civil rights, desegregated generation—people of both races reported few friends of a race different from their own, whites spoke about racism as if it were mostly in the past, blacks reported daily, ongoing struggles with discrimination, and 73 percent of blacks but only 52 percent of whites saw interracial dating as an option.[3] Perhaps most disturbingly, both whites and blacks, including those who claimed to be interested in racial harmony, spoke about race as an unbridgeable divide. "I don't know if it's ever possible for me to understand what it's like to be black. I don't know if, not having been a black growing up in the inner city, I'd ever understand," said one young white man.[4] "If you want to help me, you can to a certain degree. But don't try to understand me," said a young black woman, "because you can't understand what it's like to be black any more than I can understand what it's like to be a man."[5]

Seldom do we hear blacks saying that they can never understand whites. Blacks observe whites without themselves being seen through the veil. In this country, white survival has never depended upon understanding black people, while the reverse has often been true. This notion that we whites "can't" understand black people, however, serves the prevailing ideology and works against black liberation by identifying black people as unknowable, eternally Other. The color line and the veil that falls down upon it are not forces of nature, but inventions of culture. That veil must be lifted and that culture must change.

Race itself is an invention of culture, a social convention. On a scientific level, few of the "facts" about race that most people take for granted have any standing at all. Most scientists now reject the traditional racial classifications, at least in part because of the large number of people who do not fit into any one category.[6] Race, then, is a kind of social fiction; popular misconceptions about genetics assert a fictive biological basis for genetically arbitrary social groupings. And yet these groupings do indeed have the status of fact: "race" may not be a meaningful biological or genetic concept, but it certainly is a powerful political and social construct. The Los Angeles cops who stopped Rodney King probably didn't muse about scientific designations or social mythology before beating him bloody, nor do such thoughts even fleetingly cross the minds of the legions of white women who clutch their purses tighter when black men stand near them at crosswalks.

SOME OF THE DIFFICULTY of living as a bridge would be mitigated by company, but crossing the color line is a strangely lonely journey. Although there are now nearly a quarter-million black/white interracial marriages in the United States, usually these couples are invisible, or if visible, silent.[7] They (we) sometimes are the objects of sociological studies, with their subjectivity—what *they* think of their lives, what *their* joys and triumphs are, what *they* think should be studied—absent from those studies. Similarly, when such couples appear in literature or in film, their relationships usually are portrayed from the outside, and depicted as pathological.

What does the virtual absence, or at least the almost total inaccessibility, of a written tradition from and/or about people who have crossed the color line mean? What effects does this absence have on interracial families themselves? For one thing, interracial couples begin not as inheritors of a tradition, but as pioneers. Each of us begins again at the very beginning, with few but negative guides. If we go looking for information, testimony from those who have gone before us, we find mainly cautionary tales of tragedy and loss, written from a perspective we cannot share. Portrayed mostly from the outside by both black and white observers, we find our relationships treated as sick, manifestations of deep-seated racial myths or rebellions against our families, backgrounds, cultures: the black partner is in flight from blackness, a victim of internalized racism and white supremacism; the white partner is running from banality, in search of the exotic.[8] These stereotypes are so ingrained in all of us in the United States that, for *both* blacks and whites, there is an automatic presumption of underlying pathology in interracial relationships. To most liberal outsiders, such relationships make a retrogressive political statement, while to conservatives, they represent an alarming, sick-by-definition result of integration.

Questioning the origins of this presumption of pathology, one inevitably arrives at the intersection of segregation and normative whiteness. I do not plan to review the history of black and white sexual or romantic relationships in this country, as that is beyond the scope of this book, and the history is available elsewhere.[9] Let me note, however, that white male enslavers did enforce strict separation of white women and black men, while at the same time raping black women. In both cases, the reasoning was the same: white women and all blacks were the enslaver's property, and he wished both to increase his property (through producing more black children) and to insure that this property would be passed on to his white progeny—hence the absolute necessity of prohibiting sexual liaisons between black men and white women. The slave system rested on spurious biological definitions of race, with the entire ideology of this system predicated on the notion that black people were not fully human, an idea incorporated into the Constitution with the so-called three-fifths compromise, in which each black person was counted as three-fifths of a white person. As sociologist Patricia Hill Collins puts it, "Since children followed the condition of their mothers, children born of enslaved Black women were slaves. Forbidding Black men to have sexual relations with white women eliminated the possibility that children of African descent would be born to white mothers."[10]

To many white people, judging from my students' comments over the years and public dialogues about the persistence of poverty among blacks, slavery seems long ago and far away, best forgotten now in the interest of racial harmony and certainly not useful in the search for explanations of contemporary inequalities between blacks and whites. In *And We Are Not Saved*, however, legal theorist Derrick Bell suggests through his fictional lawyer Geneva Cranshaw that the "unresolved contradiction [between principles and ideology] embedded in the Constitution and never openly examined, owing to the self-interested attachment of some citizens of this nation to certain myths," is in fact "the real problem of race in America."[11]

Various states' laws forbidding interracial marriages were upheld by the Supreme Court as constitutional until *1967*, a full fourteen years after the Court's decision in *Brown* v. *Board of Education* asserted that separate facilities are "inherently unequal" (basically outlawing segregation). It was therefore neither long ago nor far away when the Court struck down a Virginia statute barring interracial marriage. In short, for more than a century after the end of legal slavery, laws devised to protect enslavers' interests continued to hold sway because those interests themselves did not change with the end of slavery. Bell reminds us that "economic exploitation, rather than an abhorrence of interracial sex, was the real basis for all the so-called anti-miscegenation laws. . . . These laws were motivated by the cultural advantage they secured for whites. . . . [Their basic purpose was] refusing blacks the opportunity to become the economic peers of whites."[12]

White supremacism may have begun as an economic imperative, but it has always also had both political and cultural dimensions. As Cornel West points out in *Race Matters*, culture is not "an ephemeral set of behavioral attitudes and values," but a *structure* related to the structures of the economy and politics.[13] The doctrine of white supremacism teaches that *all* people will prefer white partners, and that the white woman is the most desirable object of all—hence the enduring image of the black man pursuing the white woman.[14] The "colorstruck" black person, particularly the black man, presumably acts on internalized white supremacist values. Our society operates in such a way as to put whiteness at the center of everything, including individual consciousnesses—so much so that we seldom question the centrality of whiteness, and most people, on hearing "race," hear "black." That is, whiteness is treated as the norm, against which all differences are measured. The all-pervasive effects of this country's normative whiteness include persuading people that everyone is white unless labeled otherwise and that all spouses are of the same race. At the same time, this country's contemporary ideology of race encourages whites to believe that very little is race-related: slavery is long over, segregation and discrimination are in the past, and the persistence of poverty among blacks must be due to black people's individual or collective defects. The social and economic success of a few blacks is made highly visible and used to deny systemic racism.[15]

I run through all this here in order to ask, and to answer, a fairly simple question: whose interests are served by the attempt to portray all interracial relationships as pathological? Black critics of interracial relationships sometimes cite concern for the future of their race if increasing numbers of black people "marry out," but I would argue that ultimately objections to interracial marriages serve the interests of white supremacists. The silencing of interracial couples and the invisibility of such couples except as aberrant objects of study both serve to prop up white supremacist ideology, including the desirability of racial segregation. If interracial couples in fact have few problems apart from those shared by same-race couples and those imposed from the outside, and can lead lives as happy and healthy as any other married people's, then another barrier to crossing the color line, or erasing it altogether, crumbles.

Interracial marriages do indeed make some sort of political statement, whether intentionally or not, but this statement is not necessarily the one that is most popularly read into them. Although I doubt that most people marry in order to make a political statement, marriage is, after all, a political institution, as is racial ideology and race itself. Perhaps, like marriages between partners of any race, some or even most of these marriages are pathological; the point about interracial couples, in general, is: we don't know. In the absence of direct testimony from the inside, we *know* almost nothing about interracial marriages, although we may fantasize a great deal.

I can think of only a few films and literary works that attend sympathetically or even nonjudgmentally to the subjectivity of one or both of the principals in an interracial romantic relationship, and almost all of these postdate the racial crises in my own life. Two deeply sympathetic films, which came out in 1992, *Zebrahead* and *The Crying Game*, were made by white males and are most interested in the white male partner's perspective on the relationship. Further, the former is about teens and the latter is set in the context of the Irish-English conflict—circumstances quite different from adult marriages in the United States. David Bradley's *The Chaneysville Incident* and Octavia Butler's *Kindred*, novels by black authors, mostly offer the black partner's perspective, which inevitably is quite different from the white partner's.

Although neither Butler nor Bradley is primarily interested in tracking the psychological changes that occur in their white characters as a result of crossing the color line, both do delineate some profound changes. What is really missing for me in both *The Chaneysville Incident* and *Kindred*—and this is not a criticism of the novels or of their authors—is children. The interracial couples in these novels are childless, with neither author choosing to examine the special complications of having children.

Children change everything, I think. Further, black and white people who are willing to tolerate interracial relationships frequently draw the line at these couples reproducing, often disguising their hostility behind a mask of concern: "It's the children who suffer." There are a few books that do present interracial couples as parents—Jane Lazarre's *The Mother Knot* and *Worlds Beyond My Control*, Mark and Gail Mathabane's *Love in Black and White*, Hettie Jones's *How I Became Hettie Jones*—but for the most part, the principals in interracial marriages with children have not told their own stories, or if they have, those stories have not survived.[16] Even the Mathabanes' book says little about parenting, perhaps because they wrote this book when their children were quite small and therefore they had little experience as parents. Similarly, albeit for different reasons, Jones's powerful memoir treats mothering only sketchily. Lazarre's two wonderful novels, which have been enormously important in my life, examine much more thoroughly the particular issues involved when interracial couples have children.

With children, the dynamics of interracial marriages entirely alter. Before the first child's birth, both partners share equally in violating social norms: each has married a taboo person and each faces cultural consequences for choosing the forbidden. More significantly, perhaps, each partner is equally surprised by this choice and unprepared for those consequences. Doug, for instance, did not grow up planning to marry a white woman, just as I did not grow up planning to marry a black man. When as children we imagined our adult futures, those fantasies included partners of our own races when any partners at all appeared. Other options seldom occurred to either of us, and when they did they occurred only briefly and then outside the domain of purely private fantasy. Both Doug and I remember talking to our mothers as preadolescents about interracial marriages in what probably was a widely shared, fleeting dream of racial harmony. In the mid-1960s, when we were children, we each thought that the world's racial problems might be solved if *everyone* intermarried and thus produced a new generation in which everyone was the same blended race. Apart from this simple solution to prejudice—to which both of our mothers said, "Yes, that might work"—neither of us seriously considered crossing the color line as a personal possibility. When our fantasies included children, mine were white and Doug's were black. And that is where our adult realities diverged: Doug's children *are* black, but so are mine.

Doug always expected to be the father of black children, and was prepared for what that would mean. Despite social changes in the thirty years since Doug was Sean's age, the elements of educating a black child to live in a racist society have not changed much at all. Doug, then, can pass on to Sean (and soon, to our daughter Ailis) what his family taught him about resistance and survival and what he has learned through experience; there is a tradition for him to draw upon. There is no parallel tradition for me, the white mother of black children. For the most part, I'm making it up as I go along, becoming a bridge for my children between the white and black sides of the color line. This book is, in part, a record of that invention, and a contribution to a tradition for other white parents of black children. This book is meant also for other readers in many different circumstances. My hope is that this record of my own coming to racial consciousness through raising my children across the color line will help to clarify some of race's multiple meanings in the United States today and thus will contribute to an ongoing public dialogue about racial liberation.

When a short article I wrote about my experiences as the white feminist mother of a black son appeared in the Sunday magazine section of an eastern city's newspaper some years ago, I received a number of responses, each disturbing in its own way. There were several anonymous cowards, who sent venomous letters condemning my "crimes" and detailing black people's supposed moral and intellectual deficiencies. The creepiest of these letters began with a denunciation of racism, and then went on to explain, semiliterately, why white people should fear black people: "Why shouldn't elderly white ladies be wary of their purses when the statistics bear out the fact of the objects of black street muggings—The weak and innocent. So don't accuse whites of stereotyping—better to stereotype and be safe." These letters frightened me, their only half-conscious hatred scorching their pages. Would such hatred be satisfied by the mere writing of letters?

In some ways, though, the most troubling responses were the kindly, well-meant ones that cast my son as a victim. These letters sent me back to the original story to see whether I had portrayed my son in this way. True, I had described several racial incidents, but I did not see us as victims, and pity was the last response I had wanted or expected when I wrote the piece. I think that this type of response sprang from racism as surely as did the anonymous letters. The difference was that my anonymous correspondents were at least partly aware of their racism, while my pitiers did not recognize their own. What but a belief in the inherent superiority of whiteness over blackness would prompt someone to make the black = victim equation? I do not see myself or my children as victims, and had not written a narrative of victimization. I see myself as strong and proud, and my children as inheritors of a long tradition of survival and resistance. I see all of us as constructive agents in the world, not as passive victims. In writing, I was looking for allies, not pitiers.

And yet, perhaps I had conveyed in that article some of the discomfort and uncertainty I continued to feel about my own racial position. The summer after Ailis was born, I approached the Sagamore Bridge that spans the Cape Cod Canal with some trepidation, wondering if I would feel a resurgence of that old panic and mentally making contingency plans should the panic recur. Halfway across the bridge, I realized that the phobia was well and truly gone. I felt not only relief, but a great, limitless sense of freedom, up there in the air over the boats and barges. Living as a racial bridge can be frightening, but it can also be wonderfully freeing and endlessly instructive.

2
Starting Out

WHEN I MET DOUG, I was twenty-one, newly graduated from college, and I did not yet fully know that I was white; Doug, in contrast, knew for a certainty that he was black. Knowing that, he also knew that I was white. To paraphrase Thurgood Marshall, outside of his own house, Doug never had to look in a mirror to see that he was black. I, on the other hand, had been looking in mirrors for twenty-one years without recognizing my whiteness. And yet I was far from blind to racism, had read widely in black literature and history, and was deeply committed to the ideal of black liberation. If this is a paradox—awareness of racial inequality and commitment to its end alongside almost total lack of awareness of the meanings of whiteness—and it is, it is one that many whites live with every day, with no discomfort.

It was only when I stopped being white, in some sense, that I began to understand what whiteness means in America. Under South African apartheid, the white partner of a black person was reclassified as "colored": legally, in other words, there was no such thing as a white/black marriage. Although we do not live under apartheid, a de facto reclassification happens here, too, I think: the white partner, in learning what being black in America entails, learns what whiteness means and loses or abandons at least some of that whiteness. Being white—unless you are an out-and-out racist—usually does not include any consciousness of whiteness as a social signifier, as a state with meanings of its own. Because whiteness is treated as the norm, identical to humanity, whiteness does not get marked as a category in most white people's lives. We do not think of white writers, for example, as a subcategory of the general category of "writer," although we do mark black writers this way: writer = white, much as mother = female . . . it simply goes without saying. To say someone's cultural background is white is to say nothing at all. As Richard Dyer points out in his essay on representations of whiteness in film, "White," this (false) sense of whiteness as a natural norm is an important component of white power, which "secures its dominance by seeming not to be anything in particular," by pretending to be invisible.[1] Making whiteness visible, becoming aware of whiteness as a social construction, moves one out of the mainstream of whiteness.

I *look* white, but that white skin conceals my inner life. This feeling of being costumed in one's own skin, of "masquerading" as white in public, may be the one thing white partners of black people, and especially white parents of black children, share regardless of other differences among us. Hettie Jones, the former wife of Amiri Baraka, says that she felt "misrepresented, minus a crucial dimension" when she went to work in a white office, without her husband and children. Jones quotes a white friend with black children who calls this feeling being "disguised in your own skin."[2] Similarly, out in public without her family, Jane Lazarre's protagonist Julia in her novel *Worlds Beyond My Control* feels "masked, colorless."[3] A white woman married to a black man, Julia walks alone through Manhattan feeling "like a woman disguised, one of those Halloween creatures with skin of some otherworldly green. Blacks treat her with short-fused hostility that has become ordinary on city streets, on buses, in banks. Whites murmur confessions of racial prejudice, thinking she is one of them."[4] Out without my family, I also feel disguised. In all-white groups, I feel like a secret spy, like Ralph Ellison's character who says "our [blacks'] life is a war" and claims he has been "a spy in the enemy's country ever since I give up my gun back in the Reconstruction."[5]

The process does not work the other way, however. The black partner does not become white, does not acquire white privilege, does not describe that feeling of masquerade, has *always* been a spy in the enemy's country. The color line is permeable in one direction only.

TO EXPLAIN HOW I BECAME a racial bridge for my children, I need to explain how I came to marry a black man. The truest (and least satisfying, I realize) explanation is: I did not marry "a black man," I married Doug. Doug and I were friends before we became lovers, and therefore we knew a lot not only about about each other, but also about each other's family and friends, well before we violated the great social taboo against interracial romance. Neither of us planned to fall in love with the other—who can plan such alchemy?— and we only talked about what crossing the color line might mean for us after it happened.

Much as I would like to believe that race played no meaningful role in Doug's and my initial attraction to each other, much as I want to say that love knows no color, of course race *must* have been important in some way. But in what way? And how to separate race's role from everything else that contributed to our finding each other? Nearly two decades later, excavating the layers of our relationship, especially those first heady months, seems impossible. Both of us were young and naive, and each of us separately accounted for the other's race in a purely negative way, as in "I don't care about race, my lover's race doesn't matter." But our races helped to make us what we were—and are—and so in that sense it *was* race that brought us together.

My daughter, nearing her second birthday, asks "why" about everything and sometimes says to me, "You love me, Mommy.

Why?" Why indeed? "Because you are you," I tell her truthfully, which usually satisfies her. I want to make a parallel move here, saying I love Doug because he is Doug, and yet I know that is an inadequate explanation. Looking back, I recall that I was first attracted to Doug's calmness and gentleness, his intelligence, his dry humor, his physical self-confidence, his whole way of being in the world, and of course his race was part of all that. Having always felt like an outsider of sorts in the white lower-middle-class and working-class community in which I was raised, and later feeling appalled by the heedless attitude of entitlement I sensed in my wealthier college classmates, especially the white men, I found in Doug a kindred spirit. Having to confess the rest fills me with anxiety, but: my parents valued nonconformity, and encouraged all of their children to question authority. I was always rebellious, *never* did what I was expected to do—which caused me endless trouble in school—and so I imagine now that one aspect of my attraction to Doug was the unexpectedness of our alliance. This was not a revolt against my family, but in some way an accord with my family, in the "us against the world" way in which I was raised.

We didn't expect objections from our families, nor did we get any. And, yes, I know this is hard to believe. When near or even complete strangers discover that I am married to a black man, they often feel free to ask highly personal questions, with the first one usually some version of "What did your parents say?" This question springs from the assumption that all white people would object to a child's marrying across the color line. My parents loved Doug, but my mother *did* briefly object to our marrying. "Oh no," my mother said, "now you'll never finish your Ph.D." And a minute later: "But he was raised Protestant! You won't ever come back to the Church." After I assured her that marriage did not mean the end of female ambition and that I *never* planned to return to the Catholic church, that was the end of objections. Doug's race simply never arose as a "problem," although both of my parents certainly saw *racism* as a problem. I automatically doubt white people who claim to have grown up in nonracist families, and so I know that claiming to have had no trouble from my family is particularly hard to accept. It is the truth, however.

Writing about our families, and about their reactions to Doug's and my announcement that we planned to marry, is difficult, because all four parents were profoundly private people. My father-in-law often told me stories of his youth in the South, but few of these stories were directly about him. Far more of them were stories about things he witnessed or heard about, in which he played no central role and whose meanings for him one was left to puzzle out. This kind of storytelling seemed to run in the males of both families. My father told me many tales of his youth in Dublin, yet he never directly told me most of the salient facts about his family. For instance, I did not know until 1984, when at age twenty-nine I asked him to rough out a family tree, that the man I had believed to be his foster brother was his biological brother, an "illegitimate" son his mother had between marriages. Only then did I learn that it was this child's birth that had caused a rift between my grandmother and her older children, who self-righteously accused her of immorality, which in turn was why my father didn't know or want to know his older brothers. Similarly, we learned only this year that Doug's father had many aunts, uncles, and cousins scattered throughout the South—not so earthshaking unless you know that for thirty-something years, my father-in-law told his children that they didn't have any relatives on his side except for the few cousins they already knew.

The peculiar reserve displayed both by my father-in-law and by my father has cultural roots, I believe, indicated by parallel folk expressions. African Americans call it "putting your business in the street," as in: "That fool [usually white] puts *all* her business in the street." My father, a Dubliner, called it "telling the neighborhood," as in: "Now, will you please stop telling the neighborhood our family business." Some of the impetus toward silence in both cases comes from the experience of oppression, in which nothing, including individual consciousness, is admitted by the dominant group to be any dominated person's own. Silence and secrecy can be read in these contexts as forms of resistance, as ways of asserting the right to some kind of privacy. I think that these expressions are also rooted in fear and shame: if you tell the neighborhood/put your business in the street, you risk revealing something that can be used against you.

My mother and Doug's mother are far less reserved than our fathers were, although they too harbor secrets. Yet our mothers are also more committed to passing along personal stories, to conveying usable truths to their children; I think that they find wisdom in the personal in ways our fathers never fully shared. My mother's stories about her Dublin childhood and adolescence—tragic by most external measures but comic and wonderful by her own—taught me just about everything I needed to know to grow into an independent, tough-minded woman. My mother-in-law's stories of her youth have helped me to understand what I will need to know to mother my children effectively in a racist society. These maternal stories are private, shared late at night across the kitchen table, when just women are together: they are not meant for a public forum.

But here I am, with our parents' permissions, telling the neighborhood, putting our business in the street.

Initially, Doug and I worried that his father might be unhappy about his son marrying a white woman, but it turned out that my father-in-law did not see me as a generic white woman but as one of the many exceptions to his general rules (this one being "Stay away from white people"), so that was okay. Doug's parents welcomed me into the family, as my parents did Doug—no *Guess Who's Coming to Dinner* for us. Our siblings immediately hit it off not only with the new family member, but with the entire other family as well. Our sisters, for instance, began visiting each other without Doug and me. One of my favorite moments from our wedding came right after the service, when Doug's sister's husband turned to my brother and said, "Hey, Joe, this is great—we're brothers now!" This was no empty rhetoric, either: they have treated each other as brothers ever since. Our two families became one extended family very quickly, with everyone going away for long weekends together, visiting each other, and so on, with a friendliness and closeness I now know to be unusual among in-laws, but which at first seemed quite ordinary to me.

Race looms so large in our society that it can easily obscure our vision. Looking at Doug's and my families without the presupposition that race matters more than anything else, one can see striking parallels that could predict their good relationship. Both of our fathers were born into poverty in 1921 (Doug's father in South Carolina, mine in Dublin), lied about their ages to join the army (the segregated U.S. army for Doug's father, the Irish army for mine), rose to the rank of sergeant at age seventeen, and moved to the northeastern United States as adults. Both were skilled tradesmen, and both worked several jobs at a time in order to support their families. Both had similar prejudices—against the English of all classes and rich American whites—and similar hopes for their children. My father was more outgoing than Doug's, Doug's father was embittered in a way my father never was, and there were other differences between them. Still, the similarities are intriguing. The circumstances of our mothers' lives do not show these parallels. My mother-in-law was raised by her parents, surrounded by siblings, while my mother was given away by her parents when she was three days old, raised by a loving couple who died when she was fourteen, and was then on her own. She has eight siblings, but did not know them until she was an adult. Nonetheless, our mothers were both raised in materially and emotionally richer situations than were our fathers, both are extroverted but deeply lacking in self-confidence, both have wide circles of friends, and both have always been the emotional centers of their families. And that is really the key, I think: our families operate in similar ways, with parallel roles, and so Doug and I were raised with very similar expectations and attitudes.

Gail Mathabane asks rhetorically in *Love in Black and White*, "Isn't it every white father's nightmare to find out his only daughter loves a Negro?"[6] Well, no—it was certainly not my father's nightmare. My father's nightmare was that I would go careerist, care about money more than about people, forget my immigrant roots, become a conservative, vote Republican. Both of my parents loved Doug and treated him as their son, with my father delighting in teaching carpentry to this fifth child— having already taught my siblings and me when we were kids— and my mother mercilessly teasing Doug, just as she does the rest of us. A family joke: you're *really* part of the family when my father takes you to the hardware store and my mother makes fun of you. When my father knew he was dying, in 1992, he said good-bye to me like this, "You've always been a good daughter and I'm proud of you. I'm glad you have Doug and the children. I couldn't have picked a better husband for you or son-in-law for me if I'd done it myself."

Although several interracial couples I know have excellent relationships with their extended families, most of the people I know in interracial families have had some trouble with relatives. Mark and Gail Mathabane are perhaps more typical of interracial couples than are Doug and I in this one way. Our friends Teresa and Larry, for instance, have never been acknowledged by one of Larry's older brothers, who decided Larry was no brother of his after Larry married a white woman, Teresa, ten years ago. Usually, the white relatives object most strenuously. My friend Pat, a black woman married to a white man for about six years now, has had some difficulty with both sides: her cousins objected to her marrying white, while her sisters-in-law still treat her like an outsider. One of the sisters-in-law tried to talk Pat's husband out of his marriage plans, saying he was obviously "deranged" to consider marrying a black woman. Most of my black women friends say they would not consider marrying a white man, in part because they assume they would be inviting in-law trouble.

Doug and I were also lucky with our friends, although we did have some unpleasant surprises. Happily, these surprises were so few that they remain vivid in memory nearly two decades later. The most painful of these incidents happened with a white man to whom I had been very close—or so I thought— for five years, the last few months long-distance, as Paul had moved to New Hampshire. I had been seeing three men—Doug and two white men—for several months, and had only recently begun seeing Doug exclusively. Paul was getting married and having a small, informal reception, to which he urged me to bring a guest. I resisted, saying I preferred to come alone—I've always thought that bringing a date to a wedding makes no sense—but Paul was insistent. Finally I agreed, and said I would bring Doug. Long silence on the other end of the phone, then Paul said, "Oh, I forgot you were going out with Doug. Why not bring Rick [one of the white men]?" I explained that I was no longer seeing Rick, to which Paul replied, "Maybe you'd better come alone. You know it's not me, but some of my new in-laws would probably throw a fit if there was a black man at the wedding." I managed to get off the phone gracefully without confronting Paul—I didn't want to have a fight with him a few days before his wedding—but skipped the wedding and later wrote to him to say I was saddened by his pandering to the presumed racism of others. We have never been in touch since.

Doug and I *did* expect to have trouble from strangers, and here we were not mistaken. Often the racism we encountered was thoughtless, ignorant, and not necessarily aimed at Doug and me as an interracial couple. Sometimes, we laughed off racial trouble, turning it into a joke. For instance, I remember Doug and our friend Bruce (also black) taunting a nosy, racist landlord of mine who for some unfathomable reason of his own had imagined getting rid of all the black people who came to my apartment when one of my roommates moved. As the three of us walked up the outside steps, a flick of venetian blinds gave Mr. Landlord's snooping away. Doug and Bruce glanced at each other, burst out laughing, and started a singsong, "We're still here, we're still here! We're *her* [pointing at me] friends! We're still here, we're still here!" We fell up the stairs in fits of laughter, imagining my landlord's consternation. Despite the laughter, we knew that dealing with this landlord would shortly become intolerable, and I moved soon afterward.

Sometimes laughter soothed our hurt and calmed our anger. When Bruce, Doug, and I decided to share an apartment and went looking, we met with constant rebuffs that we were sure were racially based. Realtors who during telephone conversations expressed no objection to our admittedly unusual situation—two men, one woman, none married—would latch onto that as a reason for rejecting us once they saw us. Young but not stupid, we knew discrimination was illegal, but it wasn't overt enough to be indisputable, and if black folks brought charges every time they met with possible discrimination, suing would be their full-time occupation.

Finally, one morning I found a terrific apartment. The current tenants knew us, the landlady was not white, and I figured everything would be fine on the race front. Since the landlady was loath to rent to singles, I spent an hour or two convincing her that we were reliable. Once I persuaded her to consider us, I called Doug and Bruce at work to see when they could get to the apartment. Afraid that the place would be rented by someone else that day before they got home from work—it was an inexpensive, beautiful apartment in a very popular student neighborhood—both told me not to let it go. They trusted my judgment and I should take the apartment on the spot. On moving day, some weeks later, I picked up the phone in my old apartment (chez Snoopy Landlord) to the excited voice of our new landlady, "Maureen! Colored boys are in my house! They say they know you! What are they doing here?" Frazzled from packing up, I barked back, "Welcome to life, Mrs. Chu! They're your new tenants. And they're black men, not colored boys," and slammed down the phone. The three of us had a great time with this story over the years, with Doug and Bruce occasionally yelling at each other, "Colored boy is in my house! Welcome to life!" Things worked out well with Mrs. Chu, once she got over her initial shock and her knee-jerk racism, but I doubt she ever did believe that Doug and Bruce had jobs and I did not.

Most of the racism we experienced could not be laughed off. In 1978, when Doug and I had been together for just two years, I gave a paper at a regional conference for teachers of literature. Too broke to stay in the conference hotel, even at the special rates, Doug and I reserved a room at an inexpensive chain motel, where we paid cash for the room when we checked in. When we were leaving the next day, I remembered the sticker on the phone saying that local calls cost twenty-five cents, and so we stopped by the office to pay for the one call we had made. The (white) woman at the desk tried to charge us $39—the room rate—even though Doug told her that we had paid cash when we arrived. We could not find our receipt. We described the person who had been on desk duty when we arrived and asked the woman to call her to verify that we had paid. I was sputtering angrily, "I'm an *English* teacher," as if English teachers by definition never tried to cheat anyone; Doug was oddly silent. I realized later that he had immediately assumed the woman's suspicion was race-related, while it took me a while to figure that out.

As the clerk took her time about looking up the other clerk's home phone number and dialing it, Doug walked away from the counter and began examining the generic, motel-style prints on the walls as closely as if he were in the Louvre. It was early in the morning, and chambermaids began coming in to get their assignments. After what seemed like hours, the off-duty clerk answered her phone. "I'm at work," said our nemesis into the phone, "and a white girl and a colored boy are saying they paid you last night." "Excuse me," I said with a calmness that belied my real rage, "it's *black man* and *white woman*." She looked at me blankly and returned to her explanation, changing her description of me but again repeating "colored boy." I suddenly understood the origin of a cliché: something inside me snapped. I vaulted over the counter—a feat which I still can't believe I managed, considering that it was chest-high and I am not awfully athletic—and, grabbing the woman by the neck, slammed her up against the wall and snarled into her face, "It's *black*, damn you, black! Not colored! He's a *black man!*" The chambermaids began screaming, and two of them jumped up on chairs, as if I were a mouse scurrying around their ankles. An elderly white man, apparently the clerk's husband, appeared from some recess beyond the lobby and began yelling about the police. Doug peeled me off the woman, we paid again, he dragged me out to the car, and we sped off, with Doug lecturing me the whole time about exactly who was likely to get arrested and what might happen to us, and to him in particular, for assaulting an old white lady in Connecticut. We drove back to Boston at top speed, both of us shaking for at least half the way, and Doug repeating variations on the theme of "You cannot do things like that!"

The first few years of Doug's and my relationship were studded with episodes like what I think of as "the motel hell nightmare." Someone would make a racist remark within my hearing and I would launch an assault. Doug pulled my arm back more than once as I got ready to toss a drink in a bar, drove me away from a few places just as I began to curse out some racist, and hustled me off the scene of various race riots in the making. I started to feel like a maniac, unable to control myself and my new-found propensity for violence, a sort of Dr. Jekyll and Ms. Hyde for the twentieth century.

It took me some time to understand what was really wrong with my attack on the motel clerk, apart from the violence itself. Once the clerk changed her reference to me from "girl" to "woman," Doug became the sole aggrieved party. In calling him a "colored boy," the clerk was asserting her superior social power, in this case the power to name. Despite my good intentions, I acted on that same white power—in this case the power to determine which battles are worth fighting—when I continued to challenge the clerk on Doug's behalf. While imagining that I was defending Doug against racism, I was recapitulating black/white power relations in a racist system. There was no real difference between my behavior in this instance and the behavior of the white liberal Lady Bountiful types I scorned, and not much of a gap at all between me and the clerk I perceived as my opposite. In leaping across that motel counter, I became Doug's avenger and/or protector. But Doug did not need or want my assistance—he could fight his own battles, or choose not to fight them. In treating Doug as I had, I patronized him, robbed him of his autonomy, and took away his choices. Leaping to his defense was not in any way helpful or appropriate; it was merely humiliating.

Even after I recognized these facts and gained some much-needed humility by recognizing my own imperfections, I remained furious, not on Doug's behalf so much as on my own. I realize now that much of my anger at this time stemmed from my loss of advantages that I had not been conscious of possessing— the multiple perks that automatically attend white skin. What frightened me most was the blindness of my rage and the tenuousness of my self-control: fantasizing violence is one thing, but acting on that fantasy is another. I felt myself positioned always at the precipice of violence. I became so angry at the racism that I was really, deeply attending to for the first time that even very minor incidents often ignited my disproportionate fury. *Everything* seemed to me not only racially inflected, but exclusively racial. The possibility of nonracial conflict between blacks and whites simply disappeared from my mind. Even a dispute about parking spaces—common in Boston as in most cities—in which race was never mentioned, or even obliquely alluded to, seemed to be really about race. Actually, I now think I was beginning to see American society clearly for the first time, but was going too far in the opposite direction from whence I had begun. In this society, *all* conflict is in fact racially inflected, although race may be only the subtext, with the overt conflict primarily about something else. We bring our races and consequent power differentials into every encounter, whether inter- or intraracial. Everything in this society is racialized, with whites able to ignore that racialization whenever it suits them, but blacks never having that option.

Experiencing this secondhand, ancillary racism attuned me more closely to the reasons for the bitterness and hostility many blacks feel toward whites, as I began to see all whites as potentially dangerous. I also developed an enduring gratitude for the many black folks—my in-laws and Doug's old friends among them—who reached across the color line and generously welcomed me into their lives.

During the next decade, my racial education continued and I learned through hard experience, the help of black friends, and feminist books how to control my rage and to channel it into useful directions. Audre Lorde, in *Sister Outsider*, says, "Every woman has a well-stocked arsenal of anger potentially useful against those oppressions, personal and institutional, which brought that anger into being. Focused with precision it can become a powerful source of energy serving progress and change."[7] I often return to Lorde's words to remind myself of the real task: to focus my anger "with precision," to convert rage into change.

THROUGH MY EXPERIENCES WITH Doug, I learned about the other side of racism, white skin privilege, which within a few years appeared to me like a vast underground network, whose surface I initially had mistaken for the whole. In myriad ways, white people's skin color smooths our paths, making our lives easier than the lives of people of color. We can expect to find housing in any neighborhood we can afford, for example, or (if we are men) to have our qualifications for job openings taken seriously. We can blend into most crowds—in restaurants, classrooms, corporations—if we wish, or if we prefer *not* to blend in, can assert our individuality in whatever manner we choose. We can see people like us in most films, television programs, advertisements, and public life, read about such people in newspapers, magazines, and our culture's "classic" works. We seldom are asked to speak for others of our race, although we may be asked to speak for others of our group if we are Catholics, Jews, or Mormons out of our contexts.

African-American people are treated as being out of their contexts in most areas of this society.

The concept of white skin privilege is even harder than the concept of racism for many white Americans to comprehend fully, because very little in our society encourages us to examine the benefits that accrue to us strictly because of skin color. On the contrary, the dominant ideology of capitalist individualism works to obscure such knowledge, because recognition of white skin privilege undermines that ideology. If we get ahead through hard work *and* through racial privilege, then the notion of the United States as a place with freedom of opportunity obviously rests on beliefs that are demonstrably false and have *never* been true.[8]

In *Two Nations*, white sociologist Andrew Hacker tries to explain white skin privilege to his (white) readers through an imaginative exercise in which he asks us to fantasize about ourselves being forced to live as black people in America. What changes, material and psychological, would that alteration in race require? Hacker devotes a chapter to an overview of possible changes, discussing what it might be like to be black in this country. Well-intentioned as this exercise is, it does not begin to excavate the overlapping layers of privilege and lack of privilege, but touches only the surface. Derrick Bell points out that supposedly neutral government rules, encouraged by Supreme Court rulings, always disadvantage blacks. In effect, the Court "creates a property right in whiteness": every white person's first asset is this property.[9] Learning what this inequitable distribution of property means on a daily basis has been a process, an ongoing project for me.

Perhaps the greatest privilege of white skin is lack of consciousness about race: most white people are free to spend entire weeks, months, even years without thinking about race at all, or thinking of it in terms of others only. In contrast, I doubt that there are many black people above the age of six in the United States who can forget about race for even a single day.

This racial awareness, this constant consciousness, has been the biggest change in my own life and the foundation of all other changes. Although I retain my white skin and many of its attendant privileges—when I'm out without my family, anyhow—I have lost the dangerous privilege of ignorance. From the mundane to the powerfully serious, race is always *there*, in my head and in the world. It is in this sense that everything is racial. Race, I believe, operates in some (often hidden) way in every aspect of life. The very hiddenness of race's workings creates massive problems unknown before the outlawing of certain discriminatory practices. Derrick Bell calls white American attitudes "racial schizophrenia": the very same whites who welcome blacks into their lives in some roles carefully discriminate against blacks in others. Whites' racial schizophrenia exacerbates the effects of racism on blacks. As Bell puts it, "Because bias is masked in unofficial practices and 'neutral' standards, we [blacks] must wrestle with the question whether race or some individual failing has cost us the job, denied us the promotion, or prompted our being rejected as tenants for an apartment. Either conclusion breeds frustration and alienation—and a rage we dare not show to others or admit to ourselves."[10]

THANKS TO FEMINISM, I ENTERED adulthood thinking of having children as an option, not a requirement of womanhood: just because I *could* bear children did not mean I *had* to do so. Thanks to Doug's mother, who was known to his high school classmates as "the birth control lady" from the community health center, he grew up with similar ideas. Unlike many of our friends, who lived together for long periods and married only when they decided to have children, our decision to marry had nothing to do with children, but quite a lot to do with race. We were moving away from Boston, where we had lived together for three years, and heading to the Midwest. We both had major misgivings about marriage as an institution, as it was part of the very system of oppression we were both, in different ways, struggling against. However, our experience had taught us that interracial couples were not taken seriously—outside our immediate families, our commitment to each other was often treated as some sort of "phase" that would pass—and we both wanted to make a public statement about that commitment. Further, during our last apartment search in Boston, we had encountered some racial discrimination that had masqueraded as unwillingness to rent to unmarried couples, and we both felt we wanted at least nominal protection. We wanted to move to a new place with new lives, really. And so we got married.

When we decided to get married, we agreed to discuss the possibility of children later; neither of us was ready to have children, but we were both sure that our potential children's race was neither a barrier nor an incentive. Doug and I both knew people in interracial relationships who had decided never to have children because the burden of biracialism seemed to them too much to put on a child. We knew others who wanted biracial children because they believed such children were some-how more beautiful than either black or white children and they saw these children as advancing racial understanding. Both positions seemed to us not only racialist but also suffused with racism, as well as utterly wrongheaded in all kinds of ways. We had no qualms about bringing biracial children into the world, nor did we feel a missionary zeal to do so. We wanted to choose children as we had chosen each other: for themselves, whatever and whomever they might be, when the time was right. At the same time, we knew that our decision would have *some* racial dimension, even if we chose to ignore it, as in fact we did.

By most measures, the time couldn't have been more wrong when we did decide the time was right: I was in my fourth year of graduate school and had just begun work on my dissertation, Doug had recently switched not only jobs but careers, we had major debts and no financial resources, we lived far from our families, and yet . . . we were ready, indeed eager, to begin a new stage of our lives. Looking back now, I am astonished at how blithely we embarked upon our lives as parents, with what little thought and discussion we threw away all birth control. For two people who saw themselves as intellectuals and who discussed almost everything almost endlessly, we certainly did not fully examine the implications of having children, nor did we discuss our decision much until it was a *fait accompli.* I have friends who planned their pregnancies to fit into an academic calendar, who delayed childbearing until they finished graduate school and established careers, who carefully set aside money in preparation for their child's birth. We did none of these things. Aberrant as it was in our own circle of friends, this lack of forethought probably resembles the national norm. I think most people go into childbearing without much thought or with the wrong thoughts: you don't really know what questions you should ask until you actually have a child.[11]

When Sean was born, everything changed for me. I've heard mothers speak about what they did not know about motherhood before they became mothers themselves: the sleeplessness, the ways in which children impinge always on your consciousness, the simultaneous fragility and *permanence* of motherhood, the intensity of the experience, and the alteration in social status. I felt all this, and more, with the "more" mostly racial. Mothering

Sean and now Ailis is not all of my life, but it has made the greatest difference in my life. As their mother, I feel implicated in issues of race in ways I did not before their births.

Before Sean's birth, I had imagined that my seven years with Doug, extensive conversations with my mother-in-law and with other black mothers, and some books I had read on black child-rearing—along with lots of black literature—had prepared me to be the white mother of a black child, or had at least given me a clear idea of what issues would probably surface. This was a serious miscalculation: Doug was an adult when we met. He wasn't dependent on me, didn't need my guidance or protection, as I had learned so well from the motel episode. Perhaps more important, I didn't identify with Doug the way one does with one's child, didn't see myself in him, and didn't feel responsible for what happened in his life— interested and concerned, yes, but not *responsible*, having un-learned that feeling of responsibility when I discovered how racist it was. Similarly, although I had accurately guessed about some large issues, I had not considered the particular ways in which these issues would arise, and as any parent who has ever tried to explain reproduction to a small child while stuck in commuter traffic knows, the when and the where may be as important as the what. Nor had I anticipated the extraordinary intensity of my desire to protect my children, or the powerful, nearly overwhelming love I felt for them.

With Sean's birth, I felt a more intensely personal stake in racial issues. It was my own child's life that was on the line when racial equality, affirmative action, and human rights were threatened, which is every day, everywhere, in this country. I began to think of myself as part of a community of mothers, and especially of mothers of black children. From the very begin-ning, mothering Sean shifted my position in the world, giving me a new standpoint and a new angle of vision.

3

"Why Do White People Have Vaginas?"

W HEN SEAN WAS BORN in November of 1983, Doug and I had been married for four years and living in Minneapolis for almost all of that time, half a continent away from our families. My younger brother, Tom, had recently moved out to live with us, but everyone else awaited from a distance the birth of this first member of the next generation of our families.

The couples in our childbirth class and the women who were in my prenatal exercise class all had their babies before us, and every one had a boy. Both Doug and I assumed we would have a girl, based on some vague, mathematically insupportable idea about odds and just a feeling we both had. We were proved wrong when Sean appeared. When we made our calls an hour or so after Sean was born, everyone was effusively delighted, demanded photos by overnight mail, and announced various plans to fly out to us. The only odd comment came from my mother-in-law, who said, "A boy! That's *wonderful*—Daddy will be so happy! I'm relieved!" Relieved? "Oh, I probably shouldn't tell you this, but it's okay now that Sean's here and he's a boy," Marguerite said, "but Daddy said that if it wasn't a boy, he didn't care what it was." I spluttered a bit, and my mother-in-law said, "Don't take it personally, Maureen; that's what Daddy said to me, too, every time I was pregnant."

Well, *of course*, I took it personally: I am a woman, and a feminist, and objected to this valuing of boys over girls. I also was troubled by this vivid, early reminder that Doug and I would have to struggle with inequitable gender roles for our child, and to help him to resist a racist, sexist system that, on one of its axes, favored him because of his maleness. Or, more accurately, *seemed* to favor him: although maleness carries certain privileges, most of those privileges are in fact reserved for white males. Stereotypes of black masculinity—rapacious sexuality, violence, danger, threat—shorten black men's lives and mock the very notion of male privilege.

I also knew that simply resisting stifling race/gender defini-tions would not be enough: we would have to provide alterna-tives to fill the space resistance creates. In a world that offers few positive public images of black maleness, we would have to seek them out while also countering the vast number of soul-destroying stereotypes. As Ishmael Reed has remarked, the most familiar image of black men in the popular media is naked from the waist up, handcuffed, and thrown across a police car.[1] We did not want Sean to see black men in general or himself in particular through that racist lens, but I was not at all certain how Doug and I could help him to see himself through his own eyes, unclouded by racism or sexism. In addition to the obvious counter to racism unconditional love and real self-esteem pro-vide, we both wanted to foster in Sean a sense of wide possibility through carefully choosing books and toys for him, and through encouraging lots of fantasy play.

One of the simpler pleasures of parenting, we thought, would be giving Sean toys and playing with him—wrong, wrong, wrong, as we learned on our first excursion to a toy store when Sean was just a few weeks old. Because Doug and I were among the first of our friends to have children, we had not been toy shopping since we were little more than children ourselves, and we therefore had no clear idea about what toys were available. Before our baby's birth, we had decided to buy toys on a gender-neutral basis—blocks, trucks, stuffed ani-mals, and dolls, regardless of our child's sex—and to ban war toys and Barbie, for obvious reasons. We had guessed that black dolls would be hard to find, but otherwise we had given little thought to race as a factor in toy shopping. After all, what could race have to do with blocks? Plenty, we discovered.

That first trip to a big toy store was enlightening: we found aisle upon aisle of toys of all varieties in packages that depicted only white children playing with them. At most, one-fifth of the toys we saw incorporated no exclusionary race or gender codes on their packages. Even fancy yuppie toys, carefully aimed at both sexes—European crib mobiles and the like—came in packages adorned with pictures of white babies. In the doll aisle, blond, blue-eyed dolls outnumbered black dolls fifty to one, and the only black male dolls were Cabbage Patch Kids, which were new to the market the year Sean was born and almost impossible to get. In an effort to support progressive manufacturers, we tried to buy toys that showed some sensitivity to racial diversity in their packaging, but we also ended up buying a lot of things that had to be removed from their boxes before we gave them to Sean. Obviously, though, we could not control everything in Sean's life as easily as we discarded troubling toy wrappings, and we knew that he would be bombarded by images and messages quite contrary to the vision of self we hoped to foster. What effect would these images have on him? And how powerful would our parental influence be? We waited, and hoped.

AT ABOUT TWO AND A HALF OR THREE, Sean began to say things that suggested he understood both race and sex as categories—as interrelated categories, in fact—and that he was trying to figure out the principles that govern those categories. Like most preschoolers, Sean had a passion for categorization and a sometimes overwhelming desire to organize the elements of his world into a system that made sense to him. He was single-mindedly dedicated to grasping the abstract principles to be extrapolated from specific observations. Sean was a tiny scientist, Doug and I were his reference library, and the world was his laboratory.

One evening, Sean asked me if he would get a vagina when he grew up. After explaining that he would always have a penis but no vagina, I remarked that I had been born with a vagina and still have one, and that his father was born with a penis and still has that. "Your sex doesn't change when you grow up," I concluded. A series of questions from Sean followed, focusing on people we know and whether they have vaginas or penises. That was the end of that, I thought. Months later, Sean once again brought up the penis/vagina issue, but phrased it this way: "Why do white people have vaginas, Mom?" He evidently thought genitalia determined race, not sex: generalizing from me and his father, Sean assumed all black people have penises, and all white people have vaginas. I had to return to our list of friends, reiterate who had penises and who vaginas, and remind him of each person's race before Sean would believe that a penis meant you were male, whether black or white, and a vagina meant you were female, independent of race.

Racial differences were apparently more noticeable to Sean than were sex differences, and I suppose this could have been predicted. After all, we were making major efforts to raise Sean in a gender-free way, emphasizing that the only real differences between boys and girls were biological. We were supported by friends and by the enlightened day-care center Sean attended, where both staff and parents identified themselves as feminists. Perhaps most important, when he was a toddler Sean never saw commercial television. At three, he did not choose playmates or toys on a gender-appropriate basis, nor did he seem to think much about differences between boys and girls, especially in comparison to several other children we knew, who made a big deal about gender roles from an early age. Sean could see skin-color differences between Doug and me, and knew that I have a vagina and Doug has a penis. He never saw other people naked, so he had no opportunity to notice black females with vaginas and white males with penises. It makes perfect sense, then, that he would jumble everything up and figure that skin color and genitalia were linked.

After figuring out the vagina/penis issue, Sean decided that other physical characteristics were sex-linked as well, once telling us that girls have blue eyes and boys have brown eyes. This statement emerged at a very unlikely time—quite late at night when he had awakened to go to the bathroom—which made me realize just how deeply such issues concerned him. I explained that girls can have brown eyes and boys blue, and that many other possibilities exist, which Sean seemed to accept after recalling his brown-eyed aunt and blue-eyed uncle. He moved on to a different topic ("Why do I have to wash my hands if I don't touch the toilet?") and that seemed to be the end of it. As I tucked him back into bed, he said sleepily, "But boys have curly hair and girls don't," stuck his thumb in his mouth, and closed his eyes to signal the end of our discussion.

Sean's comments about race and his confusion about racial and sexual characteristics mirror social confusion. Race, unlike sex, has little to do with biology, popular mythology notwithstanding. As Henry Louis Gates trenchantly remarks, "Race is the ultimate trope of difference because it is so very arbitrary in its application. The biological criteria used to determine 'difference' in sex simply do not hold when applied to 'race.' Yet we carelessly use language in such a way as to *will* this sense of *natural* difference into our formulations."[2] Sex—but not gender—is an objective term of classification and therefore is comparatively easy to explain to a small child. Race and gender are subjective categories, social constructions, whose parameters constantly shift, change shape, mutate. Further, although both race and gender are socially constructed categories of analysis, they are *differently* constructed; consequently, understanding these constructions and resisting them requires quite different strategies.[3]

From about age three, Sean began to realize that racial differences were meaningful in some way beyond mere skin color, but he wasn't clear on what these meanings might be. For instance, he announced to me that people get darker as they get older and that dark people are older than light people. This makes sense as a general statement about the origins of humankind, but that wasn't his point. "No," I explained, "skin color isn't age-related. People come in all different colors and pretty much stay that way. Daddy was dark brown when he was little, and he's still dark brown. I was sort of pink when I was a baby and I'm still pink. You were light brown as a baby and you're still light brown." This seemed to make sense to Sean, and he moved on to another question ("Why is Big Bird yellow?").

A few weeks later, though, Sean once again said darker people are older than lighter people. I offered some examples of younger dark people (his friend Maggie, age two) and older light people (his grandfather, mid-sixties), and we laid that issue to rest, after agreeing that it's nice to have so many different shades of skin and hair and eyes in the world. Months passed with no further age/race commentary, but then one night while Doug was giving Sean a bath, Sean made a remark about "when you get old." It was the end of a long and exhausting day, and Doug jokingly replied, "I already *am* old!" Sean responded angrily, touching Doug's arm, *"That's* not old, Daddy! *That* [pointing to my skin] is old!" If dark skin doesn't signify age, then it must signify youth; Sean still wasn't willing to accept that skin color is independent of age and sex, all evidence of that independence carrying no weight with him.

As I look back now, Sean's early determination to figure out race's meaning strikes me as a nascent rage for order that rebelled against the intimations of chaos coming to him from the outside world. He was beginning to sense the social significance attached to race, and went looking for clues to explain that significance. The arbitrariness not only of racial distinctions themselves but also of race's social significance—when we think about it, using race as *the* crucial category depends on arbitrary historical choices that could just as easily have fastened on height or hair color or anything else for that matter—must have been apparent to him, and therefore Sean went looking for reassurances that the world was indeed an orderly place, with rules he could grasp. I think Sean felt that race *meant* something, and believed that meaning must attach to real, measurable, understandable differences, else the world might be terrifyingly unfathomable.

Sometimes Sean's mistakes about race and/or gender amused us, as when he first saw a program on commercial television and I had to explain advertisements to him. The short version of this long explanation was that you can't believe everything you see in ads, because the advertisers are trying hard to sell their products, not to let you know all sides of any issue. Sean snorted knowingly and said, "I *know*, Mom. Commercials are stupid. Like that ad for washing soap. Everyone knows that Moms don't do the laundry!"

Occasionally, Sean's mistakes alerted Doug and me to real problems. For instance, from his early infancy, we sought out books for Sean that showed both girls and boys engaged in various activities, rejecting books that encoded gender stereotypes. We also found books for him that featured black children in a variety of roles, not just as the background figures they too often are in children's literature. When we couldn't find books that incorporated racial diversity, we purchased stories about humanoid animals, figuring these were better than all-white texts. Then, at three, Sean started critiquing the pictures in his books. *"That's* not the mom," he'd say, pointing to the black mother in *Jamaica's Find*, or "Where's the dad?" as we looked at a page in a book about a white boy who was shown sitting on his father's lap. We realized that there was not a single children's book available that reflected Sean's family situation. Although many books showed black and white children playing together, no book that we found showed black and white people as members of the same family: in the world of children's literature we were invisible, nonexistent.

Actually, that's not quite true: searching through bibliographies of children's literature, I did find books about interracial families, but none I wanted to share with Sean. Rather like the literary and sociological treatments of interracial couples as pathological I mentioned in the first chapter, most children's books about interracial families fall into the problem/solution genre, treating interracial families as posing special problems. Most of these books are about adoption, such as Catherine and Sherry Bunin's *Is That Your Sister?*, and therefore did not reflect Sean's life. Others, such as Adrienne Jones's *So, Nothing Is Forever*, treat the initial rejection of the interracial family by white relatives—the problem—and the eventual growth of love between white grandparents and black children—the solution.[4] Although well-meant and perhaps valuable, such books were of no use to us. At that stage in his life, Sean's interracial family was simply a *fact*, not a problem, and we wanted to find materials that acknowledged or reflected that fact. Most children's books depicting relationships between blacks and whites—even nonfamilial ones—posit such relationships as problem-ridden. Generally, the white characters are at the center of the story, which focuses on their learning about blacks and simultaneously discovering the evils of racism.

In this highly theoretical age, talking about the impact of

popular culture or the uses of literature in simple terms is faintly embarrassing. However, whenever I ask students in my introduction to theory course why they are English majors, they inevitably respond with some version of "I like to read. Literature teaches me about myself and about other people." Although these students realize that literature does a lot of other things as well, this sort of comment is always their *first* response to the question. Numerous autobiographies by black writers remark on the poisonous lesson they learned as children from books that completely ignored their existence. Indeed, a recognition of literature's reflective or reinforcing function underlay early efforts to integrate African-American and women's literature into the curricula of colleges and universities. Sean's remarks to us indicated that he was certainly looking for images of himself and his world when he looked at books. At that young age, however, he doubted the books and thought they were wrong, as opposed to seeing our family as unusual, unlike others, "wrong."

Looking now for Ailis, who is fascinated by books, as well as for Sean, we have found exactly one "nonproblem" book about interracial families—Sarah Garland's *Billy and Belle*, which a black librarian at our local library put aside for me because she thought Belle resembled Ailis—and few about blacks and whites together in any kind of relationship that do not centralize the white child's consciousness. This may be one reason that Sean now most often reads fantasy books featuring characters that are other than human, such as Brian Jacques's Redwall series and J.R.R. Tolkein's Hobbit books. Toni Morrison has described her writing of *The Bluest Eye* as partly motivated by her need to write the book she wanted to read; I am convinced that this same desire, this hunger, for self-affirming, truth-telling tales fuels the current boom in black women's literature. Adult children of interracial couples will have to write their own books, as their experience is not only marginalized but totally erased in currently available children's literature.

My unsuccessful quest for children's literature that reflected Sean's daily environment paralleled my own search for child-care books that seriously addressed issues of race and gender, and that did more than merely acknowledge the existence of interracial families—sadly, few books did even that much. The books that addressed race progressively (such as James P. Comer and Alvin F. Poussaint's *Black Baby and Child Care*) said little about gender, while the books that addressed parents like us who wanted to avoid reinscribing traditional gender definitions (such as Letty Cottin Pogrebin's *Growing Up Free*) said little about race. At the same time, I continued to hunt for fiction for myself that depicted interracial relationships, and found very little other than tragic tales of sorrow, loss, and death. Even fewer of the few exceptions I found included children, and I was hungry for information about this crucial part of my life. I needed something to rub up against, to give me some sense of history, of shared experience. Jane Lazarre's *The Mother Knot* was the only book I found that gave me what I needed, and the sheer *relief*, the amazing exhilaration I felt while reading Lazarre's book taught me how deep my need was. In looking for literature that reflected my family's circumstances, I was looking for visibility, for verification of our existence, in some sense. Of course, that was exactly what Sean wanted, too, and our absence from literature—and from movies, television programs, catalogues, and even toy boxes—obviously worried him.

TELEVISION PRESENTS PROBLEMS akin to those of literature, but its pervasiveness and its consequent power in shaping consciousness are more troubling. We have always closely supervised Sean's television watching, restricting him to a maximum of four hours weekly of "approved" (by us) shows, with few of these on commercial television until very recently. Nonetheless, Sean absorbed a lot of information about television from other children. At three, for instance, he often played "He-Man," a game he learned at day care from children who watched the cartoon. The superhero's cry—"I am the Master of the Universe!"—lost something between television and day care, as Sean would run around the campus of the college where I then taught, shouting, "I am the Master of the University!" He learned about violent characters, about gender divisions (She-Ra certainly had a subordinate role to He-Man in the games), and about consumer culture. Once, when we capitulated to Sean's insistent wish that we go to McDonald's, we discovered that he wasn't interested in the food, but in the toys that came with Happy Meals. As we drove home from that lunch, Sean playing happily in the back seat with his toy, he cried out, "Collect them all, Mom! Collect them all!" Television's effect even on a nonwatcher clearly was profound.

Television's erasure of race's importance, even in the current crop of shows featuring black characters, blatantly serves conservative ideology, as of course the common depiction of women as objects also does. As a medium, television sends out two conflicting messages, both comforting to whites: (1) race does not matter because blacks are just like whites and have the same life chances as whites (never, of course, that whites are just like blacks); and (2) blacks are naturally completely different from whites, and are therefore dangerous enemies of civilization. In either case, black liberation efforts are irrelevant, just as feminism is portrayed as irrelevant. Television is really *for* white viewers, I think, with most programs teaching all of us how to be white and to desire whiteness. Even some supposedly progressive children's programs on PBS incorporate prevailing race/gender hierarchies. *Sesame Street*, for instance, portrays a variety of racial possibilities, but sharply limits gender roles: all of the really lovable, active muppets are male. *Mister Rogers' Neighborhood* is notably pale, and reproduces familiar gender codes as well. To give PBS its due, *Reading Rainbow*, which Sean loved, gave him a wonderful black male image in LeVar Burton, who consistently came across as an intelligent, thoughtful man who loved to read and who could learn to do *anything*, from hot-air ballooning to scuba diving. I wish there were even one program aimed at small children with an equally positive black female image. *Where in the World Is Carmen Sandiego?* has Lynn Thigpen as the Chief, but the program is aimed at an older audience. Nevertheless, Ailis and I sometimes watch it with Sean just so that she can see a strong black woman (and a multiracial group of children whose intelligence and knowledge are applauded) on television. Movies made for children, including critically acclaimed Disney animated features like *The Little Mermaid* and *Beauty and the Beast*, tell the same old story: boys *do* while girls *are*; if you're white, you're right, and if you're black, get back.

Although our first impulse was to ban all television watching and to allow few movies, Doug and I realized that such a radical approach might easily backfire and make television seem even more desirable due to its forbiddenness. Instead, we tried to help Sean to develop a critical consciousness about television, watching television programs with him so that we could talk about what we saw instead of allowing him to consume these images passively. As critic Manthia Diawara argues, adult black filmgoers are often "resisting spectators," rejecting the racial codes of Hollywood films and avoiding identification with those films.[5] Children do not have the critical repertoire and psychological sophistication that enable some adults to resist seductive screen images, but I believe even small children can be taught the rudiments of resistance.

Once, during a commercial for the construction toys he has always loved, Sean turned to me and said, "Isn't it funny that they only show white kids in this ad? They should come to our house and take pictures of *me* playing!" Sometimes Sean completely resisted the message ads sent, appearing oblivious to the implications of certain commercials. For instance, at age four he had a big collection of "My Little Pony" figures, yet never commented on the fact—apparently did not even notice—that all of the commercials we saw for these toys showed only girls playing with them. Arriving at day care one day with several of these ponies grasped in his hands, Sean was met at the door by a boy who said scornfully, "Those are *girl* toys! Are you a girl?" Sean, seeming surprised, replied, "No, I'm a boy—I have a penis," which effectively silenced his critic. As the other child walked away, Sean cast me a look that said, "Is that kid weird or what?" and ran off to play with his friends.

The fundamental miscommunication in this incident—Sean was talking about sex, while the other child was talking about gender—worked to Sean's advantage, as Sean's ignorance of gender requirements continued to do for several years. Sean did not fully recognize gender codes *as* gender codes until he was six or so, and even then dismissed them as "stupid." But then, beginning in second grade, Sean occasionally came home from school with stories about playground disputes that were rooted in gender. Several boys insisted on sex segregation, and persistently tried to limit soccer games to boys. This posed a major problem for Sean, because one of his closest friends was a girl named Rosa.

Sean did not want to participate in anything from which Rosa was excluded, yet he also enjoyed soccer and wanted to play. At seven, Sean was confronting his first major ethical dilemma, which brought with it a painful contradiction between what he learned at home about gender and what most other people took for granted. One part of this was easy: he knew, deeply and unswervingly, that he was right in his belief that sex should not be the basis on which one chose friends and that sex had nothing to do with playing soccer. I was glad that Sean did not revise his ideas to conform to those of the majority, yet being right did not get him and Rosa into the game.

Sean mulled over the problem alone for a few days, and then asked for Doug's and my advice. When we talked about the options open to him, Sean hit upon a possibility that had not occurred to Doug or me: he would speak with the teacher to see if there could be a playground rule about no exclusions from big games. He believed it was okay for two or three children to play together without having to include others—"sometimes you just want to be with your best friends," he explained—but thought that big games like soccer and kick-ball should be open to everyone. The analogy that led him to this view was the rule on birthday parties: there was no classroom requirement that everyone be invited to all parties, but there was a rule that invitations could only be distributed in class if everyone were invited. Smaller parties had to be organized outside of school. Similarly, valentine cards were an all-or-none proposition. Sean figured that games played during recess should be subject to the same strictures, on the grounds that school property—the ball and the field—was used.

Sean's inventive solution to the soccer problem skirted the controversial issue of gender entirely and centered on the uncontroversial problem of hurt feelings. It worked, too, and both Sean and Rosa got to play soccer, albeit only briefly: after all the angst, it turned out that Rosa did not especially like soccer and did not want to play after a few weeks. This was *her* choice, however, and left Sean free to play soccer when he wished without being disloyal to Rosa.

Two years later, the gender boundaries seemed even stronger and enclosed a much smaller territory, but Sean was then the veteran of numerous gender-based conflicts and seemed to take them in stride. Last spring he told me that some of the boys at school were making fun of him for playing with trolls. Apparently there was a new commercial on television that said something like "Girls like nice, cute, little trolls, but *boys* like Battle Trolls!" A few boys were using this commercial to tease Sean and other boys who liked all kinds of trolls. Our dialogue:

SEAN: I *hate* those stupid commercials, because now some kids are saying only girls play with trolls.
ME: Which kids say that?
SEAN: Well, not the girls and not most of the boys, either. Just Bill and some of the other guys who think they're real macho—which is pretty funny, because they're not macho at all!
ME: Sean, what do you think "macho" means?
SEAN: Oh, you know: tough and able to beat people up and that kind of stuff, but they're not macho, they're *dumb* and just need to think there's something special about them, so they get into saying who can do what and trying to find something they can make fun of. I'm smarter than they are, and I'm bigger so they can't beat me up, plus the teacher would go crazy if they ever even tried to fight someone . . .
ME: What do you do when they tease you?
SEAN: Ignore them, mostly, or else turn it into a joke.
ME: How do you feel when they tease, honey? Are your feelings hurt?
SEAN: No, but they can be aggravating, I guess.

ME: Well, it's hard to be different and to make your own choices about what you like. If you wanted to stop the teasing, what would you do?

SEAN: I guess I'd pretend I didn't really like trolls, which is what George did—he told Bill his mother *makes him* bring trolls to school! But I'm not going to do that, Mom—they can tease me if they want, but I'm not going to let them run my life like that. I think they should think about why they worry so much about everyone else's business! Maybe they'd have more friends and better stuff to do if they didn't spend all their time trying to get people to be like them.

I look across the table at my nine-year-old son and am so proud of him that I'm speechless. I don't think I had Sean's courage at nine, or his total lack of interest in peer approval, although I do have both of those traits as an adult. After a minute of companionable silence, I say, "Sean, I think you are pretty terrific!" He looks puzzled—why the drama?—and then says, "You are, too, Mom. We're a lot alike." Sitting there with Sean, I realize that he is right about our similarities, even in ways he probably is not considering. Socially, we are both in the "insider without" position: people who do not want unearned, false privileges and who prefer the difficult but rewarding task of making up our own lives as we go along to the comparative ease of accepting long-standing rules.

IN AN INTRODUCTORY WOMEN'S studies course that I was teaching at the time of the troll controversy, my students and I discussed Suzanne Pharr's

"Homophobia as a Weapon of Sexism." To drive home Pharr's points that lesbian baiting is used to keep women in line and that any woman who steps out of line is vulnerable to being labeled lesbian, with all of the consequent losses (of employment, family, safety, and so on), I invented a sexual harassment scenario that culminated in the harasser spreading a rumor that his victim was a lesbian. Telling my students to imagine themselves as the victim, I asked, "What would happen as a result of this rumor? And what would you do?" Together we came up with a variety of possibilities for both heterosexual and lesbian victims, none entirely pleasant or satisfying. After class, one student lingered to talk with me. She had been mocked by both men and women friends for her interest in women's studies and had been asked the inevitable question, "Are you one of those man-hating lesbians?" She was baffled about how to handle this lesbian baiting, and said, "Ever since the beginning of this class, I've been wondering: how do you turn yourself into somebody who doesn't care what other people think?"

I immediately thought of Sean: how *did* he become that kind of person so young? Where did that strength come from? Sean does indeed care what other people think; however, for him "other people" are not the general public, but the people he loves, and even they come after his own opinion of himself. Sean's near-imperviousness to peer pressure can sometimes be maddening, as it's just about impossible to convince him to do anything that doesn't fit with his notion of what he should do. On the other hand, Doug and I don't have to worry about his following someone else into trouble. Any trouble he has is his own trouble, invented by himself.

I didn't have a good answer for my student, except to say that understanding the illusory nature of certain privileges helps, as does being committed to living one's own life, not someone else's conception of that life. And love helps, too.

I HAD GROWN USED TO thinking of myself as the mother of a black son, and then I had Ailis and realized that my perspective was probably going to shift again. When I was pregnant with Ailis, and knew from amniocentesis that I was carrying a girl, many friends and acquaintances made some version of this remark: "*Now* you'll understand what I've been trying to tell you—girls and boys are really different!" In fact, I never imagined that girls and boys were the same; I did, and do, believe that girls and boys are treated differently, which creates differences in their behavior and outlooks.[6] Further, race and gender—although differently constructed, as I noted earlier—are constructed *together*: individuals learn to be black males or white males, black females or white females, not race-neutral males or females or gender-neutral blacks or whites.

Gender and race are not additive, but simultaneous, constructs, which is why "race first" or "gender first" politics make little sense. Ailis's birth made new issues certain. Until then, there was a certain symmetry in our family: both my son and my husband are black and male, so there was a fairly unproblematic link between them, in terms of modeling. Now we have an asymmetry: my daughter is female, like me, but black, not like me; black, like my husband, but female, not like my husband. Who will be her role model? What will be more salient, race or gender? My guess is that Ailis will perform a balancing act on the race and gender axes, as indeed Sean does.

A friend, Sylvia, recently told me a story that raises the problem of modeling. Sylvia, a white woman, was out doing errands with her black adopted daughter, Michelle, then five. Michelle was in the back seat, playing with a "magic" wand and pretending to transform the world. Sylvia asked, "If you really had magic, what would you do?" Michelle responded without a moment's hesitation, "I would turn your skin brown." Surprised, Sylvia bumbled around for a response and finally said, "It must feel funny sometimes to be in a family where we don't all have the same color skin." Michelle promptly burst into tears, sobbing inconsolably for ten minutes or more. Later, Michelle begged Sylvia not to tell anyone what she had said, clearly feeling that her outburst was shameful. Sylvia thinks that Michelle just felt too noticeable, too obvious, and wanted to blend into the crowd somehow. Her family looks even less like the pop culture norm than does ours, as Michelle has two white mothers, Sylvia and her partner, Anne.

Given all the psychoanalytic emphasis on identification with the same-sex parent, I wonder if Ailis, too, will long for a black mother; I must assume that at some points in her life, she will. Joanne Braxton, in *Black Women Writing Autobiography*, asserts that black women inhabit "a realm of shared knowledge communicated from generation to generation, both through literature and the oral tradition. . . . Education in black womanhood begins in infancy with lullabies, nursery rhymes, and children's games [and] intensifies during adolescence when older black women initiate younger ones in their secret recipes, sayings, and the ways and wisdom of holding a man."[7]

Braxton, I think, misses the most important elements of black mother-daughter teaching, which is less about "secret recipes" and "holding a man" than about balancing the skills required for physical survival with the quite different skills necessary to transcend the social boundaries that attempt to hem black women in.[8] Much of this teaching is not overt, but implicit in the example of the mother's life, and even direct teaching draws on mothers' own experiences, according to the section on motherhood in sociologist Patricia Hill Collins's *Black Feminist Thought*. And this is one area in which I am obviously inadequate. My life cannot provide Ailis with examples of a black woman's resistance and survival. I believe Ailis will learn some aspects of black womanhood from her black women relatives; none of them, however, lives with us on a daily basis. I will be Ailis's bridge to womanhood, for the most part, and both Doug and I will have to help her to resist the limiting race and gender stereotypes rife in our culture.

This resistance, and the positive alternatives we will offer, will of necessity take a different form from what we have done with Sean: few privileges, illusory or real, attend black femininity in this society. By temperament, Ailis is more stubborn and more demanding than Sean. She wants her way and she wants it *now*, and has already thrown dozens of tantrums in her two years of life. Sean, in contrast, threw just one halfhearted tantrum at age two and never bothered again. Ailis also loves rough play, as Sean always has, and zooms around the house on her little bike, laughing wildly as she crashes into walls and furniture without letting a few bumps or scrapes slow her down. She runs rather than walks, throws her toys around with great glee, hits people who don't do her bidding immediately, and is totally fearless. In short, at the moment Ailis is a holy terror, so it's good that she is also bright, funny, beautiful, and affectionate. The very traits that adults think are cute in a toddler, however, are likely to be seen quite differently in older girls, and especially in adolescent black girls. I don't want to see Ailis's spirit crushed by adults— particularly teachers—who reward quiet "good" girls over rowdy smart girls.

Knowing that I rebelled young against "be a lady" admonishments, Doug commented on Ailis, who had refused to go to bed and was busily dismantling a Lego building, "Well, being a lady will never be one of her problems." That is probably true, but the ladylike ideal has never been a stereotype for the mass of black women, who must struggle against quite different stereotypes that debar them from ladyhood: whore, Mammy, superstrong black woman.[9] Maybe Ailis will *want* to be "ladylike," because it is a privilege, however false, denied her, and one valued by the older generation of black middle- and professional-class people.

Thinking about the struggle against race/gender requirements and stereotypes that surely lies ahead of Ailis, I worry about the ways in which the composition of our family may present additional problems for her. For example, part of a child's coming to maturity depends not only on identification with the same-sex parent, but also on approval and affirmation by the opposite-sex parent. No matter what Doug says and no matter how deeply he loves Ailis, I fear that his marrying a white woman—me—may wound her self-esteem. I also worry about the pressure much of the black community puts on black girls and women to play a supportive role for black men, and to subordinate their self-interests to the perceived interests of black men. With troubling echoes of the 1960s—when the only place for a black woman in the Movement was "prone," in Stokely Carmichael's famous phrase—black men are now being treated as most at risk and therefore as most deserving of attention in much black political and sociological writing.[10] In the triage of racial justice, the more vivid, dramatic destruction of black men—death by violence—is again pushing the particular concerns of black girls and women into the background.

At the same time, black men are encouraged by the popular media to think of themselves primarily as victims, a stereotype as disabling as that of victimizers. Although some black men apparently accept this media-promulgated image of themselves as victims, many resist. Unfortunately, one form that resistance increasingly takes among young black men involves identifying

4

"One Drop of Black Blood"

"**L**ET ME TELL YOU ABOUT A boy I knew back home," my father-in-law begins. "Back home" is South Carolina, which Douglas left more than fifty years ago when he joined the Army at seventeen, lying about his age to get out of the South and into World War II. "This boy was *white*. I mean, he was *really* white. He was whiter than the whitest white man in America. He had good hair and everything. But he was colored, see: his mother was colored, so he was colored. Back then, if you had one drop of black blood, you were *colored*, no matter what you looked like. This really white-looking boy was colored, that's how it was. He went to the colored school, like us, and when he joined the Army, they put him in a colored unit. Some of the other guys couldn't figure out what he was doing in our unit—'What's that white boy doing in here?' they'd say—so those of us who knew him from back home had to tell them, 'He's not white, he's colored.' The Portuguese guys were a lot darker than some of us, but the Army counted all them as white. I'm telling you, though, some of those guys were *black*, even though they said they were white. But the white guys treated them like they were white, you know what I'm saying? But this white-looking boy, they treated him *colored*."

Douglas sits back, not seeming to expect a response from me. His telling of this story is part of a sort of ongoing oral history of race, with my father-in-law the teller, me the listener, and the tales mostly about the South, in the genre I think of as "when we were colored"—as opposed to Negro, black, or African American—which is the formula with which many of them begin. This particular story probably came to mind because Doug, Sean, and I were making our first visit to the grandparents in New York with Ailis, who was still a very light-skinned baby, although certainly not whiter than the whitest white infant in America. I think Douglas was trying to remind me obliquely that regardless of her color, Ailis's race is black. Until recently, I would have agreed wholeheartedly, but now I'm not so sure. Doug and I have told Sean all along that he is racially black, and ethnically African-American and Irish-American. Sean, though, at age six began insisting that he is *bi*racial, not black.

Sean first asserted his biracialism during a dinner table discussion of a meeting I planned to attend with other parents of black children. "But Mom," he interjected, "*you* don't have black children. Why are you going?" Thinking this was a joke, I laughed and said, "So, what are you, then, chopped liver?" "No," he answered very seriously, "but I'm not black either. I'm black *and* white." Doug and I locked eyes over Sean's head. A mundane exchange of information over the spaghetti had turned into a parenting crisis. Was Sean denying his blackness? Would he prefer to be white? What might have happened to lead him to this kind of statement? What kind of trouble was he facing down the line if he refused to see himself as black? Why wasn't he proud of his race? We'd been surrounding him with countless images of black achievement and black pride from infancy, he knew plenty of black people, we had always spoken positively about blackness . . . what had gone wrong?

I, in particular, was suffused with guilt and shame, perceiving Sean's assertion as an indictment of my mothering. One of the frequently reiterated criticisms I've heard about white people raising black children is that white people cannot teach black children what it means to be a black person in this society. The National Association of Black Social Workers, for example, has opposed transracial adoption since the early 1970s on exactly these grounds. We can talk about black literature, art, history, and culture, but we do so always from the outside. There is much truth to this view, especially in terms of the absence of models: a white person cannot possibly provide a racial model for a black child, or teach him/her through lived experience how to deal with racism. Furthermore, most white people know very few black people, and so cannot rely on close friends to provide this necessary modeling. Douglas Bates's *Gift Children*, about his experiences as the white adoptive father of two black children, illustrates this point. When he and his wife adopted their daughters, they knew no black people at all. Their daughters grew up in a virtually all-white environment, never knowing black adults intimately until they were themselves adults. Our situation was quite different from Bates's, however.

I never saw myself as Sean's racial role model; his father provides that modeling, with support from a large network of black friends and relatives. I *did* see myself as instilling racial pride through teaching Sean about black history and art, and through my own appreciation of black culture, which is part of what I teach professionally. When Sean told us he is not black, but both black and white, my confidence in my mothering skills was deeply shaken. As Doug gently questioned Sean about this new self-definition, I thought back to the previous summer, when Sean had seemed to take immense pride in his blackness.

Sean was five, between kindergarten and first grade, and we were staying on Cape Cod for a few weeks, as we do each year. One night, the three of us were sitting in a restaurant, waiting for our dinners to arrive, when Sean launched into an extremely loud, seemingly unprovoked lecture on Rosa Parks, Martin Luther King, Jr., Nelson Mandela, and Oliver Tambo. At first, Doug and I were simply stunned by what Sean remembered from many sources, and sat in open-mouthed amazement as he spoke. But then I looked around and realized that Sean and Doug were the only black people in the restaurant. Had Sean noticed this and decided to make his presence felt? Was this his way of saying "I am black and I have a right to be here"? Or was he just showing off—he was also the only child in the restaurant—and arbitrarily chose this particular topic in order to do so? He'd done similar things with dinosaurs and whales, evidently enjoying the adult surprise and approval. Although showing off was surely part of it, I saw his choice of topic as meaningful, and as a political act, albeit not necessarily a fully conscious one.

The evening of the "biracial revelation," as I've come to think of it, wound up allaying some of my fears, but also beginning a revolution in my ideas about race. Sean, it emerged through discussion, was not rejecting or denying his blackness; instead, he was trying to claim *both* sides of his racial heritage. He was proud of both ancestries, and saw himself as equally African and Irish—and as more Irish than many of his white classmates who called themselves Irish, as his grandparents were straight from Dublin, whereas their families had left Ireland time out of mind. Actually, at that time Sean was less interested in these ethnic inheritances than he was in the family legend that his great-grandfather was Cherokee.

In a first-grade essay on the topic "Where My Ancestors Came From," Sean wrote that he was "mostly Indian." Another crisis! When I asked Sean about this claim, he said, "*Everyone* is black or white in that class, but *I'm* the only Indian." He wanted to be different, special, exotic even. And don't most children? I remember some of the white children with whom I grew up desperately searching their ancestries for something distinctive, trying to escape what a friend of mine calls "the dreary predictability of the dominant group." As the daughter of immigrant Irish parents in a neighborhood that was predominantly fourth- or fifth-generation Italian-American, I never felt this need. With black children, however, there is always the additional layer of complexity, the fear that perhaps they are trying to capture some of that (white) "dreary predictability." On reflection, I was pleased that being biracial seemed so ordinary to Sean that it wasn't "different" enough to set him apart from the crowd, but in the back of my head some nagging worries remained. In spite of what Sean said about why he wrote about himself as a Cherokee, I wondered how much of this desire to be "special" was rooted in a wish to be "not black."

My friend Elizabeth, who is black and whose husband is black, tells me that her daughter often questions her very closely about her racial ancestry. "She'll ask me, 'What part of me, Mommy, is Indian? Am I more Indian than black? What about your family? Your grandmother was from Ireland. Am I part white too because of that?' She does a lot of that. She'd rather affiliate with something other than black." Elizabeth knows that her child did not get her negative attitudes about blackness at home, from her parents, who indeed are very involved in the black community and enormously proud of their African-American heritage. Both Sean and my friend's daughter, Marie, like the rest of us, encounter numerous negative images of blackness every day, accompanied by positive images of whiteness. Elizabeth says, "Marie has always been able to recognize that there's a negative attached to being black. She wants to be part of this elite thing," and "this elite thing" is whiteness.[1]

When Sean was in the third grade, I ran into Elizabeth just after dropping Sean at school. I was shakily trying to hold back tears, because Sean and I had just had an ugly experience. Driving to school, we stopped at a convenience store, where there were a dozen or so black teens in the parking lot, apparently waiting for their bus to high school. As we drove into the lot, Sean rolled up his car window and locked the door. "What are you doing?" I asked him. "Those kids look scary," he replied. "They do *not!*

They look like teenagers on their way to school, for heaven's sake! Open that door!" It seemed clear to me that Sean was expressing a fear of the black youths' *blackness*—there was no other explanation that I could see. Later, a white friend pointed out to me that many young children fear teens of any race, as teenagers usually ignore but sometimes hassle them. But Sean had never shown any fear of the white teens who gather on our street; in fact, he had occasionally joined them to get skateboarding tips.

I told Elizabeth what had happened and asked for advice: what would she do in my place? In response, she told me a parallel story about Marie. It seems that every time Marie encounters a group of black people whom she does not know, she acts nervous and afraid. Elizabeth and her husband are furious about Marie's behavior, but haven't devised a workable strategy for changing Marie's attitude. Although Elizabeth did not have a magical solution to the problem to offer me, her story about Marie made me feel a bit better: if the children of black parents experience problems similar to Sean's, then those problems probably are not attributable strictly to my own whiteness.

Before Sean's birth, I knew that Doug's and my children would live an experience whose most salient factors were foreign to me: they would be black in a racist society. What I had not considered was that their experience would be equally foreign to Doug: they are not just black, but black and white. I grew up white with two white parents, Doug black with two black parents. Our children have one white parent and one black parent, a fundamentally different set of circumstances from either of ours, with challenges neither Doug nor I could have fully anticipated.

Although Doug grew up aware of race, and of racism, from an early age, he says that race didn't get talked about much at home unless something bad happened, either to a family member or out in the wider world. Despite his mother's exhortations about black pride and the example of the civil rights movement—Doug was born in 1953—the fact that blackness was perceived as a liability by white people deeply shook his self-concept every time racism jumped up and smacked him in the face when he was a child.

Doug grew up in a predominantly white town, while our friend Joanna, who is the same age as Doug, spent her childhood in a predominantly black area of Washington, D.C. She remembers thinking almost everyone in the world was black; "I thought John Kennedy was black because all the Catholics I knew were black and he was a Catholic, so he must be black. I remember the lifeguard at the pool was white and we knew she was white because she had to put that white stuff on her nose so it wouldn't burn and nobody else did that. I thought people were black because they looked like me and looked like people in my family. I had friends who were black who had green eyes and blond hair, and a lot of people in my family were all different colors." This assumption of blackness is in direct contrast to the cultural assumption of whiteness, which Joanna came to understand when she left D.C. in her early adolescence.

Joanna clearly remembers having to unlearn her habits of thought when she moved to a city in Connecticut where most of her schoolmates were white. She discovered that "the little mental pictures other people got when the teacher said 'people' or 'we' or 'humans' were not like *my* little mental pictures. They saw white people, but I had always seen black people. I figured out pretty fast, though, that blacks were the exception, not the rule."

A F R I C A N - A M E R I C A N   N O V E L S and slave narratives frequently include a racial recognition scene, in which the main character becomes aware of his/her race—usually around the age of six—through some scarifying experience that can only be understood in the context of racism. For instance, in James Weldon Johnson's *Autobiography of An Ex-Coloured Man*, the narrator/protagonist joins his white schoolmates in tormenting black children, automatically thinking of himself as white in the absence of direct instruction about his "difference." One day the school principal asks all the white children in the classroom to stand. The Ex-Coloured Man stands up, but is told by his teacher to sit down and then to "stand with the rest [that is, the black children]."[2] The child goes home from school that day in a daze, and spends a long time examining himself in the mirror before asking his mother, "Tell me, mother, am I a nigger?"[3]

Sometimes the experience is not scarifying, but jarring, such as the brilliant scene in Zora Neale Hurston's *Their Eyes Were Watching God* where Janie looks at a photograph of herself and her white playmates and at first literally cannot find herself in the picture. As she later tells her friend: "So when we looked at de picture and everybody got pointed out there wasn't nobody left except a real dark little girl with long hair standing by Eleanor. Dat's where Ah wuz s'posed to be, but Ah couldn't recognize that dark chile as me. So Ah ast, 'where is me? Ah don't see me.' "[4] When a white woman identifies the black girl as Janie, she says in astonishment, " 'Aw, aw! Ah'm colored!' . . . before Ah seen de picture Ah thought Ah wuz just like de rest."[5]

These racial recognition scenes seem to support the traditional psychological model of a primary identity established apart from race, followed later by a secondary identity rooted in race. As the authors of *Black Child Care* say in their chapter on infancy, "A positive black identity (secondary identity) must be built on an inner core of pride and positive feelings (primary identity), or it may fade away under the harsh light of life's realities."[6] Yet how can a child's self ever be separate from race and gender, as this model implies? What are these "positive feelings" related to, if not to "me," which must necessarily be *all of me*," which must therefore include race and gender?

When Sean began insisting that he is both black and white, not either/or, Doug and I resisted this way of thinking, having already been ourselves thoroughly indoctrinated into thinking of race as an either/or proposition. The binary logic of race, like all binary thinking, in which the world is perceived in terms of oppositions (white/black, male/female, reason/emotion), encodes a hierarchy, with the first term of these oppositions superior to the second.

This masculinist logic is akin to the Freudian conception of the ego as rigidly bounded and defined in opposition to what is outside those boundaries. As a feminist, I consciously rejected this way of looking at the world, but my response to Sean's perception of himself as biracial showed me that I was still trapped in binary logic. Patricia Hill Collins points out that this binary logic, or dichotomous thinking, is related to objectification: "In either/or dichotomous thinking, difference is defined in oppositional terms. One part is not simply different from its counterpart; it is inherently opposed to its other."[7] Collins argues that a black feminist theory begins in a "both/and" conceptual stance, which resists the divisions created by "either/or" thinking.

Binary logic is encoded everywhere in our society. For instance, a seemingly endless parade of forms has required us to choose a single race for Sean and now for Ailis: they can be officially black or officially white, but not both. These forms usually offer the option of "other," but officialdom—as represented by the Census, day-care applications, school applications, medical records, all following the lead of the federal government—does not recognize "biracial" as a category, nor does it allow one to choose more than one category. The one exception to this general rule that I have seen is not so much an exception as an addition. A school's instructions for filling out a racial classification form notes that parents have requested their children be designated "multiracial." The instructions continue, "We respect this request, and we have included this category in our new student record system. . . . We ask, though, if you choose 'multiracial,' that you *also* select one of the five federally-defined racial/ethnic designations" (emphasis in original). The school's concession to parents' wishes takes place within a federal system that continues to ignore reality.

This demand that everyone be neatly classified into self-contained, unitary categories both reflects and reinforces ordinary social practices; by and large, people in the United States perceive race as a stable, unproblematic classification. The Supreme Court has until recently insisted on an even more rigid categorization. A person filing an antidiscrimination suit was required to pick either a sex *or* a racial category—in other words, the kind of interactive discrimination that black women regularly face was not recognized in the law: either one was a woman *or* one was black. Insisting upon a biracial identity destabilizes racial categories and points up their arbitrary nature. If one is neither black nor white, but *both* black *and* white, then the boundaries between racial categories are shown to be fluid rather than rigid. Such fluidity threatens the racial status quo and, in a racialist and racist society like our own, undermines the basic assumptions of both blacks and whites—including blacks and whites who object to that racial status quo, like Doug and me.

Most people not only cling to rigid racial classifications, but they are made uneasy by people who don't appear to fit neatly into the category in which they belong in ordinary social usage.

One day at a beach, I noticed eight-year-old Sean standing in waist-deep water with another boy and pointing toward the blanket where Doug and I sat. When I asked him later what that was about, he explained that the (white) boy had asked him if he were black or white—the other child's very first question, before name, age, or invitation to play together! Sean went on, "I said 'both.' The kid said 'You can't be *both*. Which one are you really?' So I said 'both' again, and told him to look at my parents for proof."

And this desire to "fix" race is not exclusive to whites, either. Looking at a photo taken of Ailis a few hours after her birth, my brother-in-law has just one question: "Will she darken up?" My husband is annoyed—everyone else has made the appropriately complimentary noises—but when he tells me about Mark's comment, I just laugh. After all, I had the same question myself about Sean eight years before.

When Sean was born, he was extremely light-skinned, with the nearly transparent Irish skin of my family. The nurse who came in to take birth certificate and medical record information after Doug went home to get some sleep never asked me about race. I was surprised, then, to see a typed draft that gave both parents' races as white. The nurse was even more surprised when I wrote in the correction.

I worried a lot about Sean's paleness until he was about a year old, when he "darkened up" enough to be recognizably African-American. He, at least, was born with curly hair, whereas Ailis was just as pale as Sean, but had straight hair as an infant. My worries with Sean came from a vague notion that some things would be easier for him if he *looked* black, based on my (then) belief that he was indeed indisputably black. Over the years, I had witnessed the struggles of our friend Joanna, a very light-skinned black woman, who was often mistaken for white by both blacks and whites.[8] Having been Sean's mother for nearly eight years before Ailis was born, I was less worried about her, and definitely less committed to an unreflecting belief in the stability of race.

T H E R E ' S   B L A C K ,   A N D   T H E R E ' S not-so-black, and the not-so-black often garner highly problematic privileges from the not-black-at-all. When Sean was not yet a year old, a photographer planning a billboard for a Minneapolis business asked me if Sean could be his model. At first I was thrilled and flattered. Doug and I thought Sean was beautiful, of course, but here was disinterested confirmation. The more questions I asked, however, the less pleased and the more angry I became. The short of it was that Sean was a desirable model because he was "black, but not *too* black." The (white) photographer couldn't understand why I objected to this description as racist, and was bewildered by my angry refusal to let Sean be used.

Colorism, which of course is an offshoot of racism, remains powerful among both blacks and whites. The heroines—that is, the objects the heroes desire—of many recent black films, for instance, are light-skinned, straight-haired, European-featured, all-but-white in appearance. Damon Wayans's 1992 movie, *Mo' Money*, features a pale, green-eyed woman who is pursued by the hero (played by Wayans himself), who in turn is pursued by a dark-skinned woman the audience is cued to consider ugly. The "ugly" woman's large, full-lipped mouth is exaggerated in close-up after close-up, so that the screen seems to be full of teeth, an unsubtle marker of this woman's threatening sexuality. Her sexual desires are portrayed as both frightening (the *vagina dentata*) and laughable, ridiculous. What man, the movie asks, would be attracted to a woman who looks like "a burnt french fry," as one male character describes her?

Sitting in a small theater with an all-white audience, I found this film painful to watch and squirmed at its compendium of racist clichés. The "ugly woman" scenes enraged me, as I thought of my black women friends and of my daughter. Colorism may seem to work in Ailis's favor, but that's a kind of favor she does not need, based as it is both on objectification of women in general and on particularized hatred of black women. Oddly enough, colorism works in reverse for men in this film, with the "cool" black men all comparatively dark and the one uptight, running-from-blackness black man extremely light-skinned.

This film's real audience is both black and white men, and provides them with an occasion for bonding. Damon Wayans's transgressive brand of comedy, in which he takes on racism against black men, may initially obscure what is really going on in this film—a deeply conservative, colorist, racist trashing of black women. Black men are not usually a central component of the audience the dominant cinema tries to please, as most Holly-wood films are made to provide pleasure for a white male specta-tor.[9] *Mo' Money*, although apparently under the control of a black man—Wayans asserted in several interviews that this was *his* film, that he was independent of the studio that financed it—has no meaningful difference from the white film fantasies of homosocial bonding between black and white men that bell hooks describes in *Black Looks*.[10] This film participates in what hooks calls the "commodification of difference," with the Other in *Mo' Money* the very same Other of white patriarchy: the black woman.

The long and ugly history of colorism supposedly begins with whites according preferential treatment to more European-looking blacks over more African-looking blacks, or so many present-day commentators think. The authors of *The Color Com-plex*, for example, note that lighter-skinned slaves had "easier" domestic tasks while darker-skinned slaves were used as field hands.[11] However, working in the enslaver's house, performing the most intimate of services, was not necessarily easier—psychologically or physically—than any other burden under slavery. In fact, early writings by blacks suggest that light-skinned people, particularly biracial women, were subjected to extremely harsh treatment. In his *Narrative*, for example, Frederick Douglass reminds us that biracial people in the United States were virtually always the offspring of enslavers and the enslaved women they raped. Douglass says, "It is worthy of remark that such slaves invariably suffer greater hardships, and have more to contend with, than others."[12] After slavery, whiter-looking people did fare better with both blacks and whites than did darker-looking people. For instance, light skin was a requirement of admission to many elite black social clubs, like the Blue Vein Society of Nashville, where the benefits of membership included access to business opportunities.

Writing just a few years apart (1920 and 1923), those famous adversaries W.E.B. DuBois and Marcus Garvey make similar points about colorism, charging that black people have accepted racist standards of beauty.[13] The notion of "good hair"—that is, straight, and for women, long hair—that my father-in-law mentioned in his tale of the "white colored boy" quoted at the beginning of this chapter is just one of many internalized Euro-defined ideals of beauty. The consequences of this kind of colorism tend to burden black women in particular, partly because women generally are held more to unrealistic standards of beauty than men.

Patricia Hill Collins looks at a number of black women writers' descriptions of the effects of colorism on black women, she points out that the controlling images of black women influence all kinds of relationships, and she notes that exploring these images is a continuing theme in black women writers' work.[14] Although all women are objectified by standards of beauty and black men are also penalized by colorism, black women "experience the pain of never being able to live up to externally defined standards of beauty—standards applied to us by white men, white women, Black men, and, most painfully, each other."[15] She states, "Externally defined standards of beauty long applied to African-American women claim that no matter how intelligent, educated, or 'beautiful' a Black woman may be, those Black women whose features and skin color are most African must 'git back.' "[16]

bell hooks sadly and angrily comments on a preadolescent girl she knows who has dark skin and chemically straightened hair: "Despite her parents' effort to raise their children in an affirming black context, she has internalized white supremacist values and aesthetics, a way of looking and seeing the world that negates her value."[17]

A beautiful black woman student, whom I had seen around campus but never had in class, dropped by my office one afternoon last spring to ask if I knew of any writings by "black black" women about "black black" women. She was taking an African-American literature class with another professor, she confided, "and I'm sick of reading about the problems of light-skinned women. I want to read about someone like *me*." After lending her a few books and giving her a list of others, I invited the student to come back to discuss what she read. "I don't know if I'll want to talk about it," she answered. "I think you have to be a black black woman to really understand. Like when the African-American students' group has a dance, all the men rush to dance with the light-skinned women. All of us black black women are left standing around, like leftovers. Stuff like that happens all the time, and it's embarrassing to talk about. I just thought reading some stories by black black women could give me some perspective, you know?"

One of the works I recommended to this student was Alice

Walker's essay "If the Present Looks Like the Past, What Does the Future Look Like?" Walker asserts in this essay that "there is probably as much difference between the life of a black black woman and a 'high yellow' black woman as between a 'high yellow' woman and a white woman."[18] After examining colorism in life and in literature, Walker concludes that "perhaps we *can* learn something, even from the discouraging models of earlier centuries and our own time. Perhaps black women who are writers in the twenty-first century will present a fuller picture of the multiplicity of oppression—and of struggle."[19] But what about *now*? And what of black women who are not writers? What about their pain? And their anger at light black women?

A friend pats my daughter Ailis's ringlets and says to me, "You better watch out. She's going to have some *angry* little black girls pulling that hair and asking her who she thinks she is—light, bright, and mostly white. It happened to me." But my friend is in her forties; has nothing changed? Ailis's babysitter, an eighteen-year-old black college freshman, says to her, "Now, don't you be one of these snobby African-American young ladies, tossing that hair in everybody's face." She is teasing, and Ailis is not yet two, but still . . . "Rosamalín, please don't teach her that stuff," I say. "Let's hope she has more sense than to think long hair makes her better than other people." Rosamalín laughs, then answers seriously, "People are going to treat her like she's better 'cause of that hair, believe me. You'll see. Especially black men."

Since the 1960s, the reverse sort of colorism—preference for darker skin over lighter, African-looking features over European—has sometimes also been powerful. Sean and Ailis catch hell from all sides, then: they're too dark *and* too light, too European *and* too African. It's the original colorism that most rankles, though: the black hairdresser who comments on Ailis's "good hair"; the private school that admits only two minority children to its first grade, Sean and an equally pale girl, like candidates for Noah's Ark; the white photographer who likes Sean's looks because he's not "too black." This colorism suggests that blackness is something to be ashamed of, that white is always right.

Many of the black and interracial couples I know have run into color trouble with their children. My friend Elizabeth's daughter, like the child bell hooks describes, insists on having her hair chemically straightened, for instance. Another child I know is the dark-skinned adopted daughter of a white mother and a black father. The mother, Teresa, has straight blond hair; the daughter, Sarah, has kinky brown hair. Both parents have always praised beautiful Sarah's brown skin and curly hair. Nevertheless, at seven Sarah repeated on a number of occasions her wish for "pretty hair like Mom's." Teresa, who learned to do elaborate braids on her daughter when Sarah was just a baby and who takes great pride in her daughter's appearance, says that she went through the same guilty self-doubt that I did when Sean first claimed to be biracial. Despite all her praise and her genuine admiration of her daughter's beauty, Teresa wondered if perhaps she had somehow communicated a prejudice in favor of whiteness she didn't even know she had. We parents are not, however, the only influences on our children. Teresa realized that Sarah saw television programs and advertisements that clearly prefer blond to brown, straight to kinky, white to black. These messages proved far more powerful than the contrary ones Sarah heard in her own home and in her community.

Kenneth Clark's famous experiments with black children and white and black dolls in the 1950s were repeated in the 1980s by black psychologists Darlene and Derek Hopson, with the same results: black children overwhelmingly preferred the white dolls, describing these dolls as "good" and "beautiful." The Hopsons, however, showed that the attitudes displayed by the children can be changed. After calling the black dolls "good" and "beautiful" and showing care for these dolls, the Hopsons retested the children. The results this time were markedly different, with the children now preferring the black dolls. This experiment indicates that aware adults can help black children to value blackness through modeling.[20] The authors of *The Color Complex* mention that in many interviews, adult biracial children of black and white parents "all maintained that their parents had been very much attuned to color issues. Perhaps because the parents had thought carefully about the consequences of race mixing, they proved to be better equipped to handle color-related conflicts than many Black parents."[21] Like the Hopsons' experiments, these interview results suggest that awareness makes a huge difference. Parental awareness cannot counter every troubling influence, however.

The child of another interracial couple I know is extremely light-skinned and fair-haired, with no African-American features. Everyone seems to think this child is white, including Sean, who knows him from school. Once, when Doug and I were discussing minority children at the school, Sean looked up from his book at the mention of this boy's name: "*He's* not black, he's white. So what minority is he?" When I reminded Sean that he had met the boy's father, Joseph, who is African American, and pointed out that the boy is therefore not white, but the same as Sean, Sean fell silent for a few moments. Doug and I returned to our conversation, only to be interrupted by Sean's saying, "He must be adopted, then, because he's *definitely not* black at all!"

Sean isn't the only child to make this mistake. The daughter of a black friend of mine was in this boy's classroom, but on the first day of school told her mother that there were no black boys in her class. When I told my friend that Joseph's son was in there, she was taken aback. "How could she have missed him?" she wondered. I know this child's parents are at pains to help him identify as black, taking him to a church with a large black presence and involving themselves in multicultural issues at the school, but I imagine it must be an uphill struggle if others see him as white.

Even more of a problem is a child who sees himself as white, an issue that my friend Patricia, who is black, has had to deal with. Her son, evidently identifying with his white father, deeply believed he was white and did not understand, at age four, that he was a product of *both* parents, his white father and his black mother.

As I mentioned in the first chapter, race is a social construct, not a scientific one. The Jim Crow laws are gone, taking with them the most compelling legal reasons for racial designations. Nevertheless, the idea that "one drop of black blood" makes one black remains current. This formula does not work for other racial categories—one never hears that one drop of Asian blood makes one Asian, for instance—nor does the color of the rest of the blood ever get articulated, as the culturally shared assumption of whiteness underlies all racial designations. Furthermore, the norm of whiteness is treated as "pure," a laughable fiction that relies upon a willful ignorance of history. Most of the people in the world today are racially mixed—including the majority of nominally "white" people—and yet most Americans collude in a racial mythology that identifies only *recently* (within a few generations, usually) racially mixed people as biracial or multiracial. Irish-Americans, to use my own ethnic group, do not generally consider themselves racially mixed even when they have kinky dark hair and broad noses, preferring to forget the intermarriages of Moors and Irish centuries ago.

An accurate—and racist to the core—working definition of blackness in the United States now is "an individual with any known Black ancestry,"[22] which implies a corollary: a white person is one *without* any *known* black ancestry. The passive construction here obscures a question—known to whom?—that in turn points to the dual nature of racial identity. On the one hand is the external, other-defined classification based on phenotype: anyone who displays physical characteristics associated with a particular race will be treated as a member of that race, and in the case of a mixture of characteristics will be assigned to the minority group. On the other is an internal, self-defined classification based on culture: one associates oneself with a given racial group based on a sense of a shared history and culture. Given this duality, mismatches between external and internal racial identifications are possible. A person may look white but identify black, or look black but identify white. When such a mismatch occurs, however, the complex nature of racial identity tends to be simplified and distorted by others, even by thoughtful, sophisticated observers of race.

In the aftermath of the Clarence Thomas confirmation hearings, for example, novelist Itabari Njeri objected to some other blacks' claims that Thomas was "not really black" in this way: "Just because Thomas is not ideologically in lock step with the majority of blacks doesn't make him less black genetically. You can't take away his culture."[23] Njeri's first sentence suggests that race is entirely a matter of genetics (a variation on the "black blood" idea). The second part of her comment—"You can't take away his culture"—confuses the biological and the social. You can indeed take away his culture, which is exactly what people who believed that Thomas had failed the "blackness test" thought someone or something had already done. Njeri's language betrays a slippage from genetics to culture that is, I think, typical in discussions of race, and has been for a long time.

Amiri Baraka, in an essay written in the late 1960s, goes so far as to assert that culture *creates* biology. Beginning with the claim that "Black culture is alien to the white man," Baraka goes on to equate nation, identity, and race.[24] Arguing for political separatism, Baraka says "the Black Man is played on by special forces. His life, from his organs, i.e., the life of the body, what it needs, what it wants, to become, is different— and for this reason, racial is biological, finally. We are a different *species*."[25]

At a lunch in celebration of the twentieth anniversary of the African/Afro-American Studies Program at my college, one of the speakers alluded to the implications of mitochondrial DNA research by remarking, "We are all African." At the time I was teaching Steven Biko's essays on black consciousness, in which he defines blacks as "those who are by law or tradition politically, economically and socially discriminated against as a group" *and* who identify "themselves as a unit in the struggle towards the realisation of their aspirations."[26] Biko goes on to say that "the fact we are all *not white* does not necessarily mean we are all *black*," with the difference between "not white" and "black" a matter of revolutionary consciousness. Similarly, the speaker's remark that we are all African does not mean that we are all black. I asked my table-mates how they defined blackness—what makes one black? Everyone—a fiftyish black male professor of economics, a fortyish black female administrator, and a twenty-two-year-old black female student, president of the black students' association—had a different answer, ranging from "one drop of black blood" to "culture" to "self-identification."

The professor, who insisted that blackness was strictly a

matter of culture, said that one branch of his family has "gone white." Some relative began "passing" years ago, and now the family is no longer black because they are totally out of touch with what he called "the black experience." What about the case of the musical group Young Black Teenagers? I asked. This is a group of white rappers who claim that their culture is black: *are* they black, or are they simply appropriating black culture for their own uses, in a familiar pattern? If a black person can choose whiteness (the professor's family), can a white person choose blackness? Although there had been no agreement on racial definitions until this point in the conversation, the answer to this question was unanimous: NO! You have to start with "one drop of black blood."

Toni Morrison raises the vexed question of racial identity in *Jazz* through Golden Gray, an updated, gender-switched "tragic mulatto" figure. The son of a black father and a white mother— the latter the daughter of wealthy southern enslavers—Golden Gray is taken to Baltimore right after his birth in 1875 by his mother, Vera Louise, and her former slave/now servant, True Belle. Vera Louise had not planned to keep her child, but changed her mind when she saw his blond hair and golden skin. Not knowing who his father is, Golden Gray grows up thinking he is white and enjoying the indulgence of the two women. Shocked to discover at age eighteen that his father is "a nigger," Golden goes off planning to find and to kill him, indeed hoping to kill "his own race."[27] Raised to believe that whiteness is eminently superior to blackness, Golden effects a complete revolution in his consciousness when he actually meets his father. Although the rest of Golden's story is left open—what happens to a racist white person when he discovers he has a black parent?—the novel implies that Golden finally chooses blackness. However, he also places himself outside both white and black communities. By casting his lot with the novel's "wild woman"—Joe Trace's mother, a black woman who lives in a cave and has little contact with other people—Golden finds a kind of redemption, as well as a way to live with racial ambiguity.

Historically, that "one drop of black blood" my father-in-law mentioned in his tale of the "white colored boy" pollutes oceans and generations of pure "white blood": the taint of that single drop debars its unfortunate possessor from membership in the superior racial group. I am troubled that this racist definition of blackness should now prevail among black people, unless one thinks of that single drop as having undergone a radical transformation in meaning in the evolving mythology of race. Just as "black" was once an insulting way to refer to a person but metamorphosed into a positive term through the Black Power movement of the 1960s, that drop of black blood has more silently but just as radically shifted meaning. Instead of being perceived as a pollutant, the drop of black blood now operates as a symbol of the strength and vibrancy of blackness. After all, a single drop is genetically more powerful than any amount of white blood. I'm reminded of the paint-mixing scene in Ralph Ellison's *Invisible Man*, where a drop of black "dope" makes paint a more brilliant white. The metaphor is reversed in current racial definitions: a drop of black is enough to overpower a whole sea of whiteness. Another kind of black power.

Although racial pride may transform the meaning of that drop of black blood, the truth remains that this, like the "any known Black ancestry" notion, is largely a matter of external identification, based on how one is seen by others. Further, it is only a partial definition, because along with it goes the crucial, equally vexed problem of culture. The African-American soldiers sent to Somalia as part of the relief effort, for instance, learned that skin color may be far less salient than culture. These soldiers, who expected to be welcomed by Somalis as cousins returning to their homeland, were baffled by the Somalis' scorn and wounded by Somalis calling American blacks "nigger." Said one army major, "We're the same color, but we're not the same people. I just don't feel like I'm home."[28] In popular mythology, black people share a single culture; in fact there are enormous differences of nation, region, class, education, religion, and generation among blacks. Black people in the United States do indeed share a history and also the experience of racial oppression (to varying degrees, however), but conflating race, class, and ethnicity results in gross oversimplifications. And yet . . .

AT A CURRICULUM MEETING two years ago, a white teacher at Sean's school remarked that a particular book made her uncomfortable because "the characters aren't *really* black. They have brown skin, but they're not different from white characters." At first I thought she meant that the book's illustrations showed people with European features but dark skin—a common strategy among children's book publishers who want to appear sensitive to multiculturalism without genuine effort—but after I looked at the pictures and listened to the teacher explain further, I realized that she meant the characters didn't "act black," according to stereotypical criteria. I felt like angrily challenging these assumptions and exposing the prejudice hidden in them, but thought better of further cementing my reputation as a troublemaking, radical, racially paranoid parent, so I kept silent. My friend Pat, who is black and whose husband is white, cast a few "can you believe this?" looks across the table at me, but also let the teacher's comments slide. After the meeting, the two of us did a post-mortem that focused on this teacher. Where does she get off, deciding what's black? What does "act black" mean, anyhow? Does she think all black kids live in a ghetto? She teaches middle-class black kids every day; can't she see them? *What is her problem?*

Shortly after this meeting, a white woman who teaches a popular-culture course at an Ivy League college mentioned during a phone conversation that her black students were irked by the black family in *Lethal Weapon*. They told her that these characters weren't "really black," but were more like white characters played by black actors. Instead of being annoyed by this, I was interested in the students' response. What did they mean? Did they give examples? Turns out, the characters don't "act black." Only after I hung up the phone did I recognize what had just happened: I thought it was perfectly legitimate for black people to engage in *exactly* the kind of stereotyping that infuriated me when it came from a white person. If I think it's okay for black people to define who or what is black and who or what is not on the basis of their actions, I must believe on some level that behavioral criteria exist. But what are they?

WATCHING A SPOOF OF Michael Jackson's "Black or White" video on "In Living Color," Sean laughs uproariously at the spectacle of Tommy Davidson wearing pale makeup and a long, nearly straight wig. Although I think the import of most of the lyrics sails right over Sean's eight-year-old head—"I'm still a virgin at thirty-three/ Even Madonna won't have sex with me"—he gets a huge kick out of Davidson's deadly accurate send-up of Jackson's voice and movements. For Jackson's lyric "It don't matter/If you're black or white," Davidson substitutes "I don't know/If I'm black or white," satirizing the presumed impulse behind Jackson's various plastic surgeries and his ever-lighter skin tone. The basic premise of the spoof does not escape Sean, as I learn three weeks later when he asks, apropos of nothing, "So, Mom, what *is* the solution in Michael Jackson's video? Is he black or white?" When I explain that Jackson's video isn't really about his own identity, but add that Jackson is black, Sean shoots back, "That's what I thought. So why does he want to look white?" A good question, but one for which I can't immediately come up with an answer suitable for a third-grader's understanding, so I beg off with a partial truth, "I don't really know."

Obviously, I cannot be sure why Michael Jackson has headed down the cosmetic surgery road—whim? self-hatred? blind acceptance of the media's promulgation of white standards of beauty?—but I am sure that I don't want to speculate on it with Sean at this moment.[29] Perhaps Jackson is a victim of the same forces James Weldon Johnson describes in *The Autobiography of An Ex-Coloured Man*. The biracial protagonist of this novel, who goes unnamed, details his experiences with racism, including witnessing a lynching, all of which he offers in explanation for his decision to "pass," to cross over the color line and to live as a white man. Johnson's novel is set in the latter part of the nineteenth century and the beginning of the twentieth, when the advantages of white skin were surely greater than they are now. Or were they? In any case, Michael Jackson doesn't *need* white skin privilege: he has all the money and fame the world can offer. What privilege could white skin confer on Jackson now?

Passing doesn't do Johnson's Ex-Coloured Man unmixed good, either. He does live a comparatively easy, financially successful life as a white man—and certainly no longer need fear lynching—but confesses at the end of his story that he has serious doubts about the rightness of his choice:

> It is difficult for me to analyse my feelings concerning my present position in the world. Sometimes it seems to me that I have never really been a Negro, that I have been only a

privileged spectator of their inner life; at other times I feel that I have been a coward, a deserter, and I am possessed by a strange longing for my mother's people.[30]

He goes on to remark on the burgeoning racial rights movement and on his white children. Finally, remembering his earlier musical ambitions and his great interest in black music, he ends his tale this way: "I cannot repress the thought that, after all, I have chosen the lesser part, that I have sold my birthright for a mess of pottage."[31]

The Ex-Coloured Man lives in a time when by legal definition "one drop" of "black blood" makes one black; in other words, legally he is not biracial but black. Choosing his father's race over his mother's, then, means pretending to be something he cannot legally be, not simply identifying more with one part of his heritage than with the other. This masquerade, along with his feeling that black culture is more vibrant than white, results in his final understanding that, like Esau, he has foolishly cheated himself.

The language Johnson has his narrator employ here—"coward," "deserter"—suggests that relations between blacks and whites are so adversarial as to constitute warfare. Even a cursory glance at the newspaper in any major U.S. city on any given day confirms that the war is still very much on. Our house is no island, despite peaceful racial relations within it. Much as I want to protect my children from racism, I cannot. I can, however, help to arm them against it. These military metaphors do not come easily to me; in fact, I despise these terms. Doug and I strive not to reduce everything in life to race and to help Sean to notice examples of cross-racial alliances. Nevertheless, when Sean was five, he came home one summer evening from day camp full of battle stories. He described problems he and his friends were experiencing with a boy who hit them, interrupted their games, destroyed their artwork, name-called, and generally made an all-round nuisance of himself. The three of us tried to figure out why this child behaved so badly and to invent some strategies for dealing with him, but Sean seemed certain nothing would work. Why not? "He's just on the white side, I guess," Sean sighed resignedly.

The white side? Side of what? It soon emerged that Sean thought not just of his day camp, but of the wider world as divided into "sides" or "teams." The "good team" was "black" and the "bad team" was "white." The color symbolism apparently had little to do with the racial composition of each "side": the "white side" included everyone Sean didn't like, including the troublemaking boy (who is African-American), while the "black side" included a good number of white people. Sean couldn't articulate either where the notion of sides or teams came from, nor how he decided on these particular labels, but he was adamant that this system was his own invention, of which he clearly was proud. He also seemed surprised that neither of his parents had thought of this, in his view, very sensible system first; perhaps, his expression implied, we weren't quite as smart as he had always thought.

At the time, Doug found this episode amusing, but this glimpse into Sean's imagination troubled me, both because of the intensely masculinist notion of sides in life and because of the labels themselves. Sean's world view and the labels both stemmed from some combination of his elementary knowledge of world events and his positive associations with blackness. I like the associations, but I don't like my race being equated with "bad." And yet I know that I have encouraged that equation. For instance, trying to explain to Sean what a "Tom" is, I hear myself concluding, "So don't go kissing up to white folks." A problem: I *am* "white folks" and I *do* want him kissing up to me!

With what suspicion Sean views the mass of whites came home to me one morning when he was in first grade and I was driving him to school. "A Day in the Life" came on the radio, and Sean told me that he had heard that one of the Beatles had been killed. How? Who? I began telling him about John Lennon, and soon found myself sniffling. Who killed him? Why? I gave the bare facts, and Sean commented thoughtfully, "John F. Kennedy, Martin Luther King, Malcolm X, and John Lennon. It sure seems like good people get shot a lot. And it's usually white guys that do it, isn't it?" Sean leaned forward to pat my shoulder in comfort and said, "Don't feel bad, Mom, there are still some good white men left in the world, like . . . um, like . . . Johnny Clegg! He's white, isn't he?"

I N   T H E   C O N T E X T   O F   T H E long-running race war to which James Weldon Johnson's narrator alludes, "passing" as white is dishonorable, shameful, treacherous. No truce has been declared in that war, and "passing" is still shameful. Perhaps even worse than trying to look white is trying to *act* white, or "forgetting you're black," with black folk terms like "oreo" and "buppy" mocking those who are "white inside." The most laughable thing about Michael Jackson, judging from Davidson's parody lyrics, is that he doesn't know if he's black or white. The parody ends with Davidson/Jackson asking a white cop, "Can you tell me if I'm black or white?" As the cop handcuffs him and leads him away, Davidson/Jackson looks directly into the camera and says, "I guess I am black." The danger of forgetting you're black, the parody suggests, is that reality—in the person of white authority—is likely to jump up and slap you down, "put you in your place."

According to recent newspaper and magazine accounts, black

teens who are academic achievers are often ridiculed by their peers for "acting white." This is a powerful insult that surfaces every few years in the media, but I have some doubts about its authenticity, particularly in terms of its origin. Exactly whose interests does labeling academic achievement "white" serve? Not blacks', certainly. The "acting white" charge derives its power and endurance—the authors of *Black Child Care* addressed it in 1975 as a potential problem in self-concept—from its appeal to white racism, which indeed is where I think this charge originated. I am not claiming that no black person who does well in school has ever been told he or she is "acting white." My friend Joanna told me that she and her best friend, also a light-skinned black girl, were mocked mercilessly by their junior-high peers, who would call out "99! 99!" as they walked by, with "99" meaning "you're 99 percent white" and very clearly an insult.

Joanna identifies class divisions as the root of this mockery: "My mother didn't work, and we lived in a nice house, and so on. My friend's father was a doctor, they drove a Mercedes . . . I think kids figured I'd be a snob, and so they jumped on me before I had a chance to prove myself. I tried for a long time to be 'regular,' but in doing your homework, you're acting like the white kids, you're talking like the white kids." The real meanings of the "acting white" charge are obscured by the explicit, but misleading, racial reference: I think this is a *class* issue, not a racial issue. Working-class white kids who aspire to Ivy League colleges or even to any sort of higher education at all often meet a similar kind of mockery, with their peers calling them "snobs," as I know from personal experience. If black people define blackness as a single-class identity, following prevailing white practices, then middle- and upper-middle-class blacks— approximately 25–30 percent of the black population in this country—get defined out of the race.[32]

In *Raising Black Children*, authors Comer and Poussaint address the "acting white" charge twice, suggesting in both cases that class is at the root of such insults. After decrying the false stereotype that equates blackness with poverty and addressing the problems middle-income blacks may encounter from other blacks, however, Comer and Poussaint also say that these problems may in fact be the middle-income parent's fault. "You must be certain that your child is not acting out snobbery that he may have picked up from his parents' attitudes," they say in concluding their advice to the parent of a black child who stopped playing tennis because his black friends told him it was a white man's game.[33] Later, in a section on adolescent identity problems, Comer and Poussaint criticize the notion that academic achievement is white, and then say, "Black parents who have mixed feelings about being black can create severe identity problems for their youngsters."[34] The authors seem to be trying to have it both ways, arguing first that performative criteria for race are always racist and second that black parents whose children do not meet these criteria may have serious identity problems that they have passed on to their children.

This is not to say that there are no performative criteria for race among both blacks and whites. The very existence of these criteria, these blackness tests, powerfully contradicts the "black blood" definition by showing race to be a *role*, much as gender is, that one must learn and that one may play well or poorly. Popular films offer a shorthand of performative stereotypes for racial roles: Richard Pryor applying shoe polish to Gene Wilder's face in *Silver Streak* and then trying to teach him to snap his fingers and bop along to music so that the Wilder character may "pass" for black is a classic, racist example. In life, though, the criteria are more subtle, shifting constantly according to time and place. Cornel West points out in *Race Matters* that claims about racial authenticity arise in a framework of racial reasoning that needs to be questioned: "Every claim to racial authenticity presupposes elaborate conceptions of political and ethical relations of interests, individuals, and communities. Racial reasoning conceals these presuppositions behind a deceptive cloak of racial consensus."[35] West argues that we need to interrogate these presuppositions in order to shift from a vulgarly racist view of racial authenticity to a framework of moral reasoning that would take into account the great variety of views and life choices that actually exist among black people.[36]

WHEN I TAUGHT JAMES Weldon Johnson's novel in 1989—not long after the "biracial revelation" in my house—I was amazed by the level of discomfort the *Autobiography* produced in my students, although I probably should have anticipated it: this novel calls into question basic assumptions about race in a very direct way. One student was fascinated by the character's success in passing: "He must have been *great* at acting white," she exclaimed. "I couldn't do that— they'd catch me in a minute!" Most students, both black and white, focused on whether the Ex-Coloured Man had erred in passing and on the events that led to his choice; none, however, raised the problem of the notion of "passing" itself for a biracial person. All of my students thought of the protagonist as black, despite his mention of his white father and his detailed descriptions of his light skin color and his European features.

When I asked why they thought of him as black and not as biracial, there was a moment of surprised silence, followed by indignant outbursts from three of the seven black students in the class: "He *is* black!" A general murmur of agreement from most of the others, both black and white. Why? "Because he *is*! One drop of black blood, and you're black." When I probed further, trying to get students to articulate where this definition came from and why they accepted it—indeed, insisted so vehemently upon it—I was met by exasperation and circular arguments. Finally, I pointed out that this was the slavocracy's definition; wasn't there a problem with accepting it so uncritically?

The white students soon dropped out of the discussion, but the black students kept appealing to "common sense": a biracial person might think of himself or herself as both black and white, but if he/she looks black, others will define him/her as black. Even if he/she looks white—the situation of Johnson's protagonist—he/she will be seen as black by people who know of his/her black parent. Therefore, the consensus was, he/she should think of him/herself as black, because others will. And who are these "others"? Well, white people, mostly. "Okay, then," I said to my students. "You're saying that white people have the right to define race for everyone, that it's *white* definitions of blackness that we should accept." No, it's not about what's right, it's about reality: white folks may not have the right to define race for everyone, but they have the power to do so. No matter what I said or how I challenged them, the students always came back to this point, refusing even to consider seriously the political and ethical issues involved in accepting the notion that race is in the eye of the more powerful beholder, and that one should internalize this beholder's gaze.

On the most basic, getting-through-the-day level, my students were right: the reality is that anyone who looks black or has a black parent will be seen as black, and will probably perceive him/herself as black as well. Nor am I suggesting that it would be preferable for a biracial person to see him/herself as white. What I *am* saying is that to see a biracial person simply as black is to reduce complexity, to deny his/her real heritage, and to make interracial families invisible. Following Sean's announcement that he is both black and white, Doug and I made efforts to support his self-concept and to make his biracialism visible in the world. We had always emphasized his Irishness to him—even in the name we chose for him, which we saw as making visible that part of his heritage likely to be unseen by others—but we began to identify him as *bi*racial whenever the issue of his race arose. This seemed to me to be an issue of respect for Sean; he may be a child, but he still has the right to define himself as he wants. At the same time, we continued to make clear to him that the outside world will see him solely as black, and to support his positive associations with blackness.

Sometimes this making biracialism invisible is part of a fully articulated political strategy. Afrocentrist scholar Molefi Kete Asanti calls biracialism a "masquerade": "There is neither a political nor a social definition within the American society for such masquerade. Neither biracial nor interracial has any political meaning in the contemporary setting of the United States. . . . The person [who claims a biracial identity] seeks to escape the social and political definition for people whose biological history is essentially similar."[37] When Harry Allen and Chuck D of the rap group Public Enemy tell an audience of college students that there's no such thing as biracial in America, that one is either black or white, and then go on to explain that in "black" they include all oppressed races, their political ideology and strategy are manifest.

Which is not to say their position is unproblematic: the day after this talk, the students in my introductory African-American studies course were still agitated about it, and asked if we could depart from the syllabus to talk about it. That day, students spoke personally, often in a deeply moving way, about their concepts of race and their own racial identification. The four biracial students in the class testified to confusion: wanting to assert their (at least) dual heritage, but also having to "prove" to black people that they are "really black." After class, one young man walked back to my office with me, obviously still upset about Harry Allen's message. "I *am* black, I know that, but my mother is white and she is still my mother. I won't deny her just because this guy says I'm a Tom if I don't. But he's right, too, isn't he? In America, either you're black or you're not; saying you're half black is like saying you're sort of pregnant—either you're all the way, or you're nowhere at all."

The reality, however, is that you're *not* "nowhere at all." My son and daughter are biracial, but they are not half white and half black, or half Irish-American and half African-American: they are *all* white and *all* black, *all* Irish-American and *all* African-American. That is, they have the right to full member- ship in both groups, and I want to help them to insist on that right. What right do majority Irish Americans have to define black Irish Americans out of that ethnicity, for instance? Going along with the "one drop of black blood" definition props up the racist delusion that whiteness is pure, unmixed, and I refuse to countenance that white supremacist move. And I also refuse to take on the "White Mother Martyr Syndrome" by denying my role in my children's ancestry.[38] If my children do not look Irish-American, that is only because we have accepted a false image of what Irish Americans, or whites, look like. I remem- ber Gloria Steinem on her fortieth birthday announcing that she *did* look forty, contrary to "compliments" she received; pointing to her face, she said, "This is what forty looks like." Pointing to my children, I say, "This is what Irish Americans look like." Asserting Sean's and Ailis's Irishness is a political act, aimed at undermining complacent racism.

Scorn for those who straddle the color line is built into language itself: half-breed, mulatto. "Mulatto" comes from the same root as mule—in Spanish, *mulatto* means "young mule"— and a mule is a sterile hybrid, the product of a male ass and a female horse. Sean and Ailis are not hybrids, unnatural creations doomed to sterility.

Overcoming such stereotypes requires politics, and it is politics, finally, that offers a resolution to the issue of identity. The race war that Johnson's Ex-Coloured Man opts out of goes on, fought in the groves of academe, the halls of government, the offices of corporations, the schools, the streets. I don't want my children to be cowards or deserters, and so I will encourage them to love blackness and to understand that they must ally themselves with blacks—however they identify themselves—because that alliance serves social justice and human rights.

Increasing numbers of "black" people are now asserting their multiracial identity, without diminishing their commitment to black liberation struggles, as some black civil rights advocates fear.[39] I don't want my children's racial identity to be adopted by default, because of how others see them, but to be chosen because of how they see themselves as agents in the world. They are indeed biracial, but they must act on behalf of themselves and others as black. That is, although Doug and I both reject racial polarization and want to help our children to resist it, we also realize that Sean and Ailis must live in a society in which racial polarization is the norm. In order to be effective members of that society and, especially, to be workers in the struggle for social justice for all, Sean and Ailis will have to live with contradiction. In the end, they will need to affirm their blackness, while simultaneously rejecting the polarization that limits the meanings of blackness. Racial identity, finally, is not a private matter, but a public statement.

Nor is racial identity eternally fixed, chosen for life. A good friend's son is now a freshman in college. In high school he identified himself as biracial, had roughly equal numbers of white and black friends, and showed little interest in politics. Now he says he is black, is involved exclusively in campus organizations dedicated to black issues, and majors in African-American studies. He's still young, so there's no telling where he'll end up. Sean is now in the fifth grade, and I notice he refers to himself as black more often than he says he is biracial, but he also describes himself as Irish-American. Other than science books and fantasy novels, his choice of reading material these days often revolves around blackness: biographies of Benjamin Banneker, Ray Charles, and Ida B. Wells; the Brer Rabbit stories told by Julius Lester; *Black Heroes of the Wild West*; a history of slavery called *Many Thousands Gone*. He likes to wear his Malcolm X hat, which makes more than a fashion statement—or did, before white folks started appropriating the X symbol. I notice that he often tells Ailis that her curly hair is beautiful, and he recently told me and Doug that he wants to grow his own hair into dreadlocks. On St. Patrick's Day this year, Sean went off to school in a Cross Colours outfit—which he loves largely because the clothing company is owned by young blacks in South Central Los Angeles—with a pin that read "100% Irish."

5
The Fourth R

ONE YEAR TO THE DAY
after the Simi Valley jury ignited the uprising in Los Angeles by
acquitting the police who beat Rodney King, Sean reported that
an older white child on his school bus had called him "nigger."
The jury verdict and the name calling were business as usual in
this country, with both emanating from precisely the same
source. There having been no revolution in racial attitudes in
our lifetimes, Doug and I had assumed Sean would at some
stage be called "nigger" and therefore we were not surprised.
Nevertheless, we were angry, and we expected the school's administration to act to demonstrate both to Sean and to the name
caller that using "nigger" was definitely a major offense.

What happened in the aftermath of this name calling could
be a case study in how schools perpetuate racism, and the roles
of teachers, administrators, students, and parents in creating an
environment in which racism is the norm. This norm, however,
is seldom examined, usually denied, and, when confronted,
treated as an aberration.

Our expectation that Sean's school would take decisive action
in itself may appear to be a step forward; however, it is an
appearance that actually masks a lack of real racial progress. A
friend told us that Sean's reporting the "nigger" incident with
the clear expectation of some official redress and our perception
that the school would not endorse racial taunting showed that
we have all come a long way in thirty years. He said when he
was name-called in school and on the school bus, he told his
parents without for a moment expecting that the name callers
would be punished or even that his parents would inform the

school. He knew for a certainty that the school was on the side of the name callers, and that he and his family could not expect the school to defend or to protect them. His parents' response reaffirmed this knowledge: "You're better than those kids who call you names. They're ignorant. They're just trying to make you mad enough to hit them so that you'll get into trouble. Just ignore them."

While it is true that black children who were called "nigger" by whites thirty years ago had no reason to expect institutional support and that at least some black children today have quite a different view, the older generation's understanding that the schools are on the side of those who yell "nigger" reflects a reality that has not changed. What has changed is the surface only: now schools take a public position—racism is not tolerated—that contradicts their actual relationship to racism, and confuses children and their parents. When overtly racist things happen, children usually get no support from authorities; even when the racism is acknowledged, it's often treated as being of the same order of seriousness as any "interpersonal" problem, like name calling about clothing or appearance.

My friend Joanna told me that her son was called "nigger" by another third-grader in his school outside Dallas, where he is one of only two blacks in the class. Jim's response—"I am black and I'm proud of it! So you can kiss my butt!"—seemed appropriate to me and to Joanna, but not to the school's principal. The principal called Joanna, not to let her know about the racism, but to inform her about Jim's use of "bad language." When Joanna inquired further, it developed that the principal had not planned to notify the name caller's parents at all, a decision she justified by saying something like, "We all know they have a problem." Jim's lesson from this episode, then, was that it's okay to use racist language in school when you come from a racist white family, but not to use minor vulgarity when you are black.

The morning after the "nigger" incident, I reported it to the vice-principal of Sean's school, who is in charge of discipline, stressing that I expected him to act swiftly and to keep me informed about what happened. Mindful of Joanna's experience, I was not sanguine about the school's probable response, but felt I had to take a stand. During our conversation, Mr. Walsh said, "Sean is such a nice little boy. It's a shame that he has to put up with this kind of name calling." I replied, "Mr. Walsh, you're unclear on the point here: Sean does *not* have to 'put up with' this kind of name calling, and it's your job to make sure all the students know that no black child has to 'put up with' being called 'nigger.' "

While apparently indicating real concern about Sean, Walsh's comment also expressed his unreflecting belief that something unchangeable about Sean—his color—caused him to be the target of racial taunting. He surely would not have said about a victim of physical aggression, "It's a shame he has to put up with hitting." This belief is a serious error, as it is actually something changeable about society—its racism—that causes racial insults. While Mr. Walsh and I were having our phone conversation, a poem on "black" was being posted outside a classroom in the school. A line in this poem, which was written by fifth-graders, reflects the same perceptual error I pointed out to Mr. Walsh. "Black," a white child wrote, "is why Rodney King got beat up." Well, no: *white* is why Rodney King got beaten.

After we spoke, Mr. Walsh pulled Sean out of his classroom to ask what had happened on the bus. Sean told him, and Mr. Walsh asked, "Did anyone else hear this?" Yes, another child had overheard the whole exchange. Mr. Walsh went to that child next, instead of approaching the name caller directly.

When the witness confirmed Sean's account, Mr. Walsh called the accused boy's mother, whom he later described to me as "aghast" and quite worried about what would happen to her son. Then, he finally confronted the name caller and gave him a lecture about the seriousness of his transgression. "This boy is new to the school, and has had a few other problems here," Mr. Walsh confided to me later. "He's trying too hard to fit in." What a terrible comment on the school! "Doesn't it worry you, Mr. Walsh, that this boy evidently believes that name calling a black child is a way to 'fit in' to your school? Have you thought about where he might have got this idea?" I asked. Much verbal dancing around my question ensued.

The next day, Mr. Walsh again took Sean out of his classroom, this time to ask him to think about what might be an appropriate punishment. Sean came home and talked to Doug and me, giving us a very long list of things he thought should happen. After we discussed the list together, Sean narrowed it down to three chief points: (1) the child should apologize directly to Sean; (2) he should be suspended for a day (the usual consequence of fighting); and (3) while he was suspended, he should do some research and write a report on what is wrong with saying "nigger." Doug and I told Sean we were proud of him, because his list was a constructive attempt at education instead of a vengeful punishment.

Sean went off to school, ready to give the list to Mr. Walsh. However, Mr. Walsh did not inquire about Sean's thoughts and the list remained unread. Instead, he gathered Sean, the name caller, and the witness together, gave a shorter version of his earlier lecture to all three of them, required the name caller to apologize, and indicated that he expected Sean to "forgive" the name caller. Sean told me later, "I accepted his apology, but I *don't* forgive him, and I won't forget it, either. Once you've said something, you can't unsay it and you can't undo the hurt, so why should I say it's okay?" Sean was bitterly disappointed that so little had happened, and felt the name caller had not really learned anything. "Next time something like this happens, Mom," he said, "I'm just going to punch the kid in the face. At least that way he'll think twice about saying 'nigger' again. I'll probably be suspended, but I just don't care."

Both Sean and the name caller did learn some lessons from this episode, but I doubt they are the lessons Mr. Walsh consciously intended to convey. Both children learned that it is still okay for white children to call black children "niggers." The name caller apparently viewed racist language as one avenue to "fitting in," and his experience did nothing to disabuse him of this notion. The vice-principal's rhetoric aside, racist taunting was treated as an "interpersonal" problem, not as an assault by one child on another. The burden ultimately fell not on the name caller or on the school, but on Sean, who was expected to "make up" with the name caller and in that way to heal a breach he had not caused. From this, Sean learned that officialdom is unlikely to defend him, despite its claims about concern for him, and therefore he must defend himself—with fists, if necessary. Further, Sean's testimony alone was not enough to galvanize Mr. Walsh into even the mild actions he took: a "witness" was needed. Actually, I believe that a *white*, "disinterested" witness was needed. Had the child who overheard the name calling been black, or even been a white friend of Sean's, I think the outcome would have been even less satisfactory.

None of the lessons of the name-calling episode were new to me, nor do I think most parents of black children would find the other conclusions I drew from the episode surprising. Mr. Walsh was quick to blame the parents, asserting that the child must have learned racist language at home, while the parents were just as quick to blame others, specifically black people. After talking to the child's mother, Mr. Walsh remarked to me that some black people call each other "nigger," and I later learned that the name caller initially claimed that Sean had called him "nigger" first.[1] The child's mother expressed concern, but *not* concern about Sean: she was worried only about what would happen to her son. The name caller's parents never expressed dismay or regret to Doug or me—a telling omission, I think— which leads me to believe that there were no consequences for this child at home.

Mr. Walsh categorically denied that the school bore any responsibility beyond reprimanding the child. He refused even to consider that the school itself was culpable in that it had created an environment that supported racism, with black students in an isolated minority. He did acknowledge that it seemed the child had learned the actual word "nigger" in school, during a school play about Langston Hughes. The teacher may have had only the best intentions in putting on this play. Unfortunately, the contemporary school environment is not distinctly different from the environment the play was meant to critique, and so at least one student got the "wrong" message from the play.

These "wrong" messages come across in a thousand different ways every day in even nominally progressive schools, like Sean's. In the rest of this chapter, I want to use the "nigger" episode—which caused a brief flurry of activity, but really changed nothing—to explore some of the key problems I see in schools, from my dual position as a mother of black children and as a white professor in a public institution.

In *Savage Inequalities* Jonathan Kozol details the enormous gaps in quality of public education provided for predominantly black schools and for predominantly white schools, with the majority of the nation's black children "sentenced" to poor schools. Forty years after the Supreme Court's *Brown* v. *Board of Education* decision, our country's schools remain racially and economically segregated, with predictable consequences. Given that reality, my criticisms of Sean's school experiences may seem like whining, as few black children have the educational opportunities Sean's school provided—he got called "nigger" in a much better environment than most black children.

My son attended a private school with an excellent academic reputation, impressive resources, committed teachers, and involved parents. In addition to the basics of reading, writing, social studies, science, and math, Sean had computer class, music, art, gym, and industrial technology (a k a "shop"). He had daily access to a terrific school library and went on a number of interesting field trips each year, to plays, concerts, museums, and historic sites. His classmates were the children of legislators, professors, lawyers, and managers; many were wealthy, very few were poor. Yet even in this privileged environment, racism thrived. What Sean's experiences—and the experiences of other black children I know—suggest is that even when black and white children attend the same school, sit next to each other in class, read the same books, and do the same lessons, the educations they receive have quite different effects.

I first suspected this divergence might be widespread when Sean was in kindergarten. His kindergarten was part of his day-care center, whose population of teachers and students was largely black and Hispanic. This center reflected our city's school-age population, which is about 70 percent "minority." Little did we know then that within just a few years this day-care center would come to represent a lost racial paradise. We had chosen our neighborhood in part because the local public elementary school was well integrated and reputed to be the best in the city. But as we began asking acquaintances with older children their opinions of this school, we discovered a distressing pattern: the majority of white parents we asked were pleased with the school and lavishly praised the principal, while not one parent of a black child was pleased and many bitterly criticized the same principal. Both white and black parents mentioned that very few black children were enrolled in the school's gifted program, but most of the white parents explained this fact in various ingenious ways, whereas the black parents cited it as a concrete example of institutional bias. Black and white descriptions of the school diverged so radically that these two groups of children may as well have been in separate schools. And so, in November of Sean's kindergarten year, we found ourselves betraying our philosophic commitment to public education and researching private school options.

After narrowing the possibilities down to four, we began visiting schools. At every school we were enthusiastically welcomed and, indeed, pursued; I felt like the mother of a high school football star dealing with college coaches. We interpreted this interest in Sean as signifying a real, as opposed to merely rhetorical, commitment to racial and cultural diversity within these schools. As the weeks passed, we talked with other parents of children at Sean's day-care center and encouraged them to apply to the places where we were applying. We had a selfish interest here—hoping that Sean would not be in a tiny minority and that he would have a friend or two beginning first grade with him—but also more altruistic reasons: we feel that *all* black children deserve the best education available, and we then believed that, even if Sean were not admitted to the schools of our choice, perhaps some other black children would be. In the end, Sean was, they weren't. Why? I can't be sure, but I believe that this disparity was about race, color, and money/class.

The children who applied with Sean were all intelligent (they tested into gifted programs, for instance) and were evaluated similarly by their kindergarten teacher. The difference among them was that Sean was the "right" kind of black child, I think, in the eyes of admissions officers. He has a white mother, for one thing, with whom white administrators probably felt more comfortable than they did with black parents. He is light-skinned, he is middle-class in every way, his parents have comparatively high incomes. His friends who applied were darker-skinned, were of lower-middle-class or working-class origins, their parents had lower incomes than we did, and they probably would have qualified for financial aid. In other words, I believe these schools wanted Sean because he wasn't "too black" and he would not cost them money. He would "fit in" while at the same time improving their racial balance.

The school search process went on for months, and in June we still did not know what we were going to do with Sean when September rolled around. We finally decided we would take our chances with the public elementary school, where at least there were a lot of black children, rather than send Sean to a school where he would be one of very few black children. We explained to admissions officers that we were not sending Sean to their schools because they had not admitted adequate numbers of black children.

A week before the academic year began, I received a phone call from the new principal of a fifth private school, which had not contacted me after I sent in Sean's application eight months earlier. She had just been hired, and had discovered that the school had six empty slots in a first-grade class. She was calling parents of children on a waiting list to check on interest. I was interested, but wary: how many black children would be in this class? I recalled that there had been no way to self-identify as minority on this school's application, and I was concerned that this absence meant the school had no commitment at all to affirmative action. The new principal said she would happily fill *all* the slots with black children if she could discover which of the applicants were black and if their parents remained interested. "I've only been here a few days," she confided, "but from what I can see, not much attention has been given to racial diversity. I'd like to change that." Huzzah! We sent Sean to her school, and several of his friends enrolled there too.

This principal was indeed committed to racial diversity and to a multicultural curriculum. Furthermore, she saw the interdependence of the two—without substantial numbers of so-called minority children, no curricular changes will make much difference, and without a multicultural curriculum, minority children will be marginalized and alienated—and worked very hard during her tenure at the school to institute both. From the beginning, however, she was embattled, with the forces of (white) tradition among faculty and parents alike allied against her. Parents of "minority" children formed an organization to support each other and the principal. In the end we lost the principal, who was forced to resign two years after she began.

By the time Sean was in third grade, the numbers of minority children had begun to dwindle. By the beginning of fourth grade, Sean was in the position we had wanted to avoid: he was part of a minuscule minority. There were a few black girls in his class, but Sean was the sole black boy in his entire grade, and he felt the weight of this lonely-only position. We began investigating other schools, looking for a place that did not lose the black boys by fourth grade. Sean wasn't sure if he wanted to switch schools, because he had several good friends in his class. He told me in April, however, that although most of the time he didn't mind being the only black boy, sometimes he did, and being alone made it harder to tell which things were racial and which were not.

Doug and I found a private middle school that was 70 percent "minority" (46 percent black). Founded a decade ago to provide an excellent education for inner-city youngsters, the school seemed to remain true to its mission. The admissions director, a young black man, told me the incoming fifth-grade class was already filled but he invited Sean to visit on the chance that an opening might occur. The day in May that Sean spent at this school was a revelation for all of us. He *loved* the school, even though it was missing some of the amenities he enjoyed at his current school, and he begged me to call the admissions director every day to check on a possible opening (I demurred). What was the best thing about this school? "I'd *never* be alone there! The class has sixteen kids, and nine of them are black. If someone called me nigger, there'd be a whole bunch of kids to stand up for me. And the white kids probably don't say stuff like that anyway, cause their families send them to a school that has a *lot* of black kids, so they probably don't hate black people."

Two weeks later we got the good news: there was an opening, and Sean was in if he wanted to attend. Did he? "Yes, definitely. Even if [the old school] gets a lot more black kids, it will still be a white school with black kids in it. But [the new school] isn't a white school—it's for everyone," Sean said thoughtfully.

The last thing Doug and I did at Sean's now-former school was to work on a proposal to bring in greater numbers of black children. This proposal originated with our multicultural parents' group and had been in the works for nearly three years. Finally, it appeared the school's administration would act on our advice. They were galvanized into this belated action, I believe, by learning that we were moving Sean and that our friend Kadeja's daughter was right behind him, on her way out that door. For reasons that are still not clear to me, the administration called a meeting of the parents' association's executive board to discuss the proposal. The almost entirely white group objected to the very idea of bringing in more black children. "The school's test scores will go down!" wailed one officer of the association. "There will be a lot of fighting in the halls. The school won't be a safe place," said another. They either were oblivious to the racist assumptions underlying these fears or simply did not care. To these parents, the idea that blacks are stupid and bellicose was *fact*, not racist stereotype. It was a bitter end to four years that began with high hopes.

MANY PARENTS WORRY profoundly about their children's entry into school; most child-care books I've looked at address these worries in terms of the child's "adjustment." That is, parents are presumed to worry about how well the child will get along in school and how easily he/she will "adjust" to the school environment, with its rules that differ from home rules. In my experience, the worries of progressive parents, especially feminists, differ substantially from these more common concerns, as such parents do not necessarily *want* their children to "adjust" to school. These parents see widely shared social values, reflected in the schools, as conflicting with their own convictions, and do not want their children to abandon the values they have learned at home in favor of the more conservative values promulgated by the schools.

Schools begin indoctrinating children immediately. Sean came home from day care at age two and a half and announced that there was no school the following Monday because it was George Washington's birthday. Curious as to what the day-care teacher could have told a group of two- and three-year-olds about George Washington, I asked Sean why this day was a holiday. Who was George Washington? "I'm not sure," Sean said thoughtfully, "but he was some kind of parent and he sure did have a big lump of hair on his head!" Sean entertained this domestic view of George Washington until first grade, when he brought a book about Washington home from school. As we read the book together, I noticed illustration after illustration showing black people in the background. These people were never mentioned in the text. Finally, I asked Sean who he thought these folks were. "George's friends," he said. Of course, they were George's *slaves*, but this didn't seem like the right moment to impart that information.

In retrospect, I regret not telling Sean right then that Washington was an enslaver, although I later did tell him when it became clear he wasn't going to get this information from school discussions of history. My friend Joanna told me about taking her children to Mount Vernon one summer, and realizing that they had never heard about Washington's slaves:

> I had to tell the kids that our ancestors were not living in the big house, sitting around being fanned, we were *holding* the fan, or in the kitchen doing the cooking! We saw Martha Washington's kitchen and Martha Washington's cookbook, and most any kid, black or white, would have this idea of Martha in there with her apron. Martha Washington never saw that kitchen! She probably took those recipes from the black slaves and wrote them down. . . . Then the kids go back to the same questions about slavery: why? how could they [enslavers] do this? how could they get away with it? Their schools don't ever really address this stuff.

The schools do not "address this stuff" because it is not in their interest to do so. The basic problem is that schools are not set up to fight racism; they are set up to teach it. Racism is really the fourth R of the basic curriculum. Patricia Hill Collins identifies schools, along with other of society's institutions, as among the "essential sites for transmitting ideologies objectifying Black woman as the Other. These institutions are not controlled by African-Americans and are clearly the source of and ultimate beneficiaries of these externally defined controlling images."[2] I would extend this argument outward, to include the objectification of black men as well. In "Civilization and Its Discontents," Freud asserted that women were hostile to civilization and he positioned women as the Other of civilization; schools teach that civilization is *white* and by positioning black people as the Other they imply that blacks are the enemies of civilization.

With very few exceptions, schools exist not to educate, but to indoctrinate: their purpose is not to give children information that might liberate them, but to train children to occupy particular places in society and to naturalize social divisions. School curricula play an important role in this indoctrination, and what is left out of curricula teaches children key lessons about their society. Many of my black friends have offered their services as free consultants to their children's teachers, passing along materials about African-American history, donating black-oriented toys and games, and even going into classrooms to give mini-courses on African-American history and literature.[3] Although this approach does introduce children to material they might not otherwise encounter, it does not solve the problem. Children soon learn what their teachers really value: it is the material their teachers teach themselves and on which they assign homework and give tests. Everything else may be interesting, even fun, but it's an extra, like gym. When African-American materials are not integrated into the curriculum, but taught by visitors or confined to one month of the year (February—Black History Month), children instinctively understand that they are not central to their education.

African-American novels and autobiographies often include scenes of instruction, in which an adult black person discovers what was not taught—indeed, what was deliberately ignored or misrepresented—in school. In *The Autobiography of Malcolm X,* for example, Malcolm describes teaching himself black history through reading in prison, trying to find out the truth about the country in which he lives. In *Home to Harlem*, Claude McKay creates a lecture on Toussaint L'Ouverture, Africa, literature, and the Bible for a character to give the protagonist, Jake. Jake is filled with pride upon learning about the history that is his and that had been hidden from him.

Again and again, African-American literature portrays school curricula as designed to demonstrate white superiority, part of an educational system that *at best* is indifferent to black children's needs and that far more often is downright hostile. Huey P. Newton sums up his formal education in *Revolutionary Suicide* this way: "During those long years in the Oakland public schools, I did not have one teacher who taught me anything relevant to my own life or experience. Not one instructor ever awoke in me a desire to learn more or question or explore the worlds of literature, science, and history. All they did was try to rob me of the sense of my own uniqueness and worth, and in the process they nearly killed my urge to inquire."[4] This miseducation is why Newton asserts that "throughout my life all real learning has taken place outside school."[5]

But certainly much has changed since Newton was in school in the 1940s and 1950s, hasn't it? The recent publicity accorded curricular debates may leave the impression that an experience like Newton's is a thing of the past, but not much of substance has changed. Because African Americans themselves are not seen as "constitutive elements" of the American experience, to use Cornel West's phrase, African-American history and literature continue to be seen by most white educators as peripheral to their enterprise.[6] Sean has learned virtually everything he knows about African-American history and literature—in other words, about the *whole* American experience—outside of school.

During Black History Month a few words may be said about Martin Luther King, Jr., or a special program may be presented, or children may be required to write a report on a black figure. During the other nine months of the school year some teachers may assign readings by a black writer or two, but these are tiny changes. I think of this as the "add in" philosophy: leave the basic curriculum intact while adding in a few black folks.

In seventeen years of college teaching, first as a graduate student and then as a professor, in two elite private schools, a large research university, and a state college, in three different areas of the country, I have *never* encountered a student who had read more than four works by black writers or who had studied black history in elementary or secondary school. The only students who bring prior knowledge of black literature and history to my classes have gleaned that information on their own. My guess is that most recent black high school graduates could make the same statement Newton did twenty years ago.

The curriculum is one aspect of a vast problem. Children still begin learning racism from day one in school, but that racism is now often so subtle, so much a matter of the unspoken, so inseparable from the basic assumptions underlying the whole school culture that it is difficult to identify. For African-American children and their parents, conflicts with schools are often painful and resistant to solutions. In addition to having the problem of sending their children into an environment that is unlikely to reflect their family's values, these parents also must contend with the institutionalized racism their children inevitably will encounter in the school. Moreover, they are unlikely to find support from majority parents, faculty, and administrators when they try to address this racism. Douglas Bates devotes a chapter of *Gift Children* to his black daughters' experiences in schools in the 1970s and 1980s, noting that no authority figure ever identified with their position or tried to help them fight back against racism.[7] Indeed, in schools—as elsewhere in society—white people in responsible positions are usually unwilling to admit that racism exists in their environment in any form. And if the racism isn't overt—in other words, if no one is running down the halls screaming "nigger" and wearing a Klan hood—you can count on a long, uphill struggle.

Only "minority" teachers and the parents of "minority" children—whether the parents are themselves "minority" or not—can be relied upon to display any interest whatsoever in issues of race.[8] Although I agree with bell hooks that antiracist work that attempts to convince whites that they too are victimized by racial discrimination and prevented by their white skin privilege from becoming full human beings is following a mistaken strategy, I *do* think white children have much to gain from truly integrated schooling and a really multicultural curriculum.[9] I would not attempt to eradicate white privilege by arguing that the oppressors are themselves oppressed by the burden of oppressing others—a fairly common claim, particularly by men vis-à-vis women, and a delusional one, I think.[10] Although white self-interest is not directly served by eliminating white privileges, it *is* served when white children see their parents working for social justice.

In my experience, the great majority of white parents of white children operate on a highly competitive, individualistic, masculinist model of behavior where their children are concerned, irrespective of their expressed political commitments. Furthermore, even those parents who voice concern with gender equity and work to eliminate sexism for the sakes of their daughters *and* their sons tend to be blind to the ramifications of institutional racism and to see racism as a problem only for its obvious victims. In short, race in the schools is a "special interest" issue, not a concern for all parents.

By this point, I have become so used to white parents' refusal to recognize their own and their children's role in reproducing a racist society that I am unendingly, wildly grateful when whites who do not have black children are concerned about racial justice and try to do something to effect it. I realize that this gratitude is problematic—we should not be grateful when people simply do the right thing—but doing the wrong thing is so much easier, and so much more common, that I can't help but be grateful.

Nor can all parents of black children be counted upon to support collective antiracist efforts in schools. Just as not all women are feminists, not all black people are black liberationists and not all white parents of black children recognize the political implications of their family arrangements. Several of the black parents at Sean's school indulged in a kind of magical thinking, imagining that their children would somehow escape the sting of racism because of the parents' own political, social, or economic power. Several others seemed to view their children as different, special, and assumed these children therefore would not be affected by racial trouble. Both of these groups of parents operated on the same competitive, individualistic model common among white parents of white children: if their own children were not directly affected, they acknowledged no responsibility for joint action. Still others accepted the existence of racism in the school but felt powerless to change it and opted out of collective struggles. Some parents—especially white parents of black children—allowed their assimilationist beliefs or integrationist ideals to blind them to racist realities. One black friend of mine ultimately dropped out of our parents' support group because she felt the group gave her inadequate support when her daughter was assigned to the class of a teacher who reportedly had spouted racist nonsense in a fairly public forum.

SEAN HAD HIS FIRST UNMISTAKABLE encounter with overt racism at the end of first grade. A white boy in his class with whom Sean often played at school told his friends that his mother had said he could invite three children to a party celebrating the end of the school year. Sean was one of the favored three, and supposedly the boy's mother would call me to make arrangements. Each morning Sean asked me if she had called the night before, and the answer was always negative. Finally, two days before school ended, he asked me to call her. After I explained why that wasn't a good idea, from the position of etiquette, Sean decided to ask Bob if the party was still on. He came home from school forlorn. Yes, the party was on, but Bob had told him that his mother now said he could only have *two* boys and that Sean could not come.

Sean couldn't understand why Bob's mother so disliked him: "She only met me *once*, Mom, and I was nice to her!" I was present the one time this woman met Sean—at a school function—and from her look of surprise when she saw Doug, me, and Sean, it was clear that Bob had neglected to mention Sean's race. I suspected that racism was at the root of her decision to limit the party to two guests when Sean's name turned up on the list. As Sean wondered aloud about why he was excluded, Doug and I had a silent dialogue over the top of his head: should we tell him our guess?

We began by asking Sean if he remembered what prejudice was. Yes, he did, and he had a good definition: "When people treat other people unfairly because of their race or something else like that." We explained that this mother might be prejudiced against black people—a racist, in short—and this might explain why Bob wasn't able to have him to his house. Sean felt less devastated, as he no longer worried what about *him* was so awful that he couldn't go to Bob's party, and he turned his attention to what was so awful about Bob's mother. We then explained that he and Bob could still be friends at school, and that he shouldn't blame Bob for his mother's ideas—also, we reminded Sean, this was just a guess by us, not a fact. We came up with an alternate celebration for the last day of school, and things seemed okay.

Three years later, I still wonder if we did the right thing. Later experiences with Bob's mother have affirmed the correctness of our guess, and Bob and Sean are no longer friends, in large part because Bob started saying openly racist things to Sean the next year. On the way to a Black History Month program, Bob shoved Sean in the hall and said, "I'm *sick* of Black History Month! When are we going to have White History Month?" Sean, already fairly clear about curricular biases from discussions at home about my teaching and about schools generally, said he answered, "Every other month *is* White History Month, and I'm pretty tired of that!" My doubt about our handling of the end-of-first-grade episode does not stem from any sense that I may have misjudged the mother of this child but from the effect on Sean. Doug and I have tried not to label every injustice racism, because there is enough overt racism to fight without our having to seek it out. We share the caution later sounded by the authors of *Raising Black Children*, who say that "calling [injustice] all racism can make your child feel that he is drowning in a sea of ill-feeling with no allies or potential allies anywhere. It can cause black children to be fearful and uncomfortable."[11] Knowing what racism is in the abstract does *not* help one to understand what it is in the flesh, and I really didn't want my son to lose his innocence at age six. But he did.

I did mention all this to his first-grade teacher, whose response was disbelief—"I've known that family for years. I really doubt they are racist." Later I wished I had said something more to the teacher or to school administrators, as when Sean next encountered racism from a peer, we met with the same disbelief. My naiveté about white teachers surely came from my own whiteness; despite my experiences as an adult, I retained remnants of the belief that most people are basically good and that nonracists would become antiracists when presented with evidence of racism. Darlene and Derek Hopson warn the readers of *Different and Wonderful* that "non-Black school officials seldom appreciate or even acknowledge how prevalent racial discrimination, even racial attack, is in their schools, and how deeply such discrimination can affect the victims."[12]

In third grade, Sean again had an experience that he couldn't quite understand on his own. A new boy (white) entered the class midyear and was assigned to Sean's table for lunch, where previously Sean and two white boys, all good friends, had sat together. A few days after the new boy joined the group, he asked the children at the table what they planned to be when they grew up. Sean, the first to answer, said he wanted to be a paleontologist and an archaeologist. The next boy, evidently at a loss—this was not normal lunchtime chat, I gathered from Sean—said, "Me too." The new boy, Noah, turned to the white "me-tooer" and said, "*You* will probably be successful. *You* [he said to Sean] won't. *Everyone* knows that you won't get into college, and if you do, you'll flunk out." Now, Sean is a very bright child who does quite well in school—why would Noah come up with this particular analysis? After Doug and I discussed it, we agreed that the episode might well have been racially motivated, and Doug said he'd mention it to the teacher—whether racial or not, Noah and Sean obviously had some sort of problem that needed to be resolved, as this was not the first time Noah had made a cutting remark to Sean.

The teacher's instantaneous response was the usual, "I'm *sure* it was not racial!" She went on to say that Noah habitually made critical remarks about other children's intelligence, always claiming to be smarter than they. "Well, then," Doug replied, "you really do have quite a problem, which I hope you'll do something about." We heard nothing from the teacher, but Sean reported that she had gathered all four children who had been at lunch together to ask what had happened—beginning this conference with "Sean's father says that . . ."—and basically encouraging Noah to agree that his remark had nothing to do with race.

Later, I approached Noah's mother when we were both at school for a class event, hoping to discuss Sean's and Noah's mutual difficulties. At first I did not mention race. Noah's mother had a totally dismissive attitude: "They couldn't have a big problem, because I never heard of it, and Noah gets along with *everyone*." This provoked me to blurt out, "Well, he *doesn't* get along with Sean, and I suspect it may be racial."

"It's NOT racial!" she hissed furiously. "Noah doesn't notice race! Until this minute I didn't know if Sean was green or blue or what! He's probably one of these bully boys who uses his fists, and doesn't know how to use words to solve his problems!" Noah's mother saw "black boy" and thought "slow, inarticulate, violent." She did not, and *could not*, see *Sean*.

When I told this story to other parents, response split along racial lines. All the black parents saw it as a racial episode and all but two of the white parents said it did not sound at all racial to them. Noah's mother's remarks, especially the "green or blue" stuff (people don't come in green or blue, colors popular with white folks when they want to claim race doesn't matter) and her assumption that Sean had trouble with words and was given to physical violence (which accords with white stereotypes of black males), suggest to blacks that she has a race problem, while many whites don't hear them that way.

Maybe it was not racial—although it's interesting that Noah chose the *one* black child at the table as the target of a disparaging remark about future success and that his comments echoed racist views of black intelligence and achievement—but the unwillingness of most whites even to consider that it might have been racial exemplifies the problems parents of black children face in dealing with issues at school, and that black people in general face in their dealings with any predominantly white institution.

A TEACHER AT SEAN'S SCHOOL once remarked that black boys seem "rougher" than white boys and more willing to fight. She insisted that this was not a racist stereotype, but the *truth* that emerged from reflecting on her years as a teacher. The notion that "all Black boys of a certain age are bad is common in American society," as the Hopsons note in *Different and Wonderful*, and this teacher apparently brought this idea into her classroom.[13] Perhaps the boys themselves brought this idea to school with them as well, mirroring what they heard about black boys outside school. Let's assume for a minute that the black boys in Sean's school *did* use their fists more often than did the white boys—although I do not believe this is true—why might that be so? Could racism play any role in this behavior? That is, could these children feel so frustrated and so angry at their minority status and at racial attacks by other children that they *do* turn to fighting?

That was certainly once true in Sean's case. Sean, who is not a fighter, came home from second grade one day looking very bruised and scruffy. It turned out that he had been in a fistfight on the playground—which the teacher just mentioned had witnessed but had done nothing to stop—with the only other black boy in his class. Why? Well, basically because many of the other children (white) had been calling Sean "David Two" and David "Sean Two." I guess that, in order to demonstrate their separateness, the two boys ended up fighting. Doug and I were furious, both that Sean had fought and that he had allowed himself to be manipulated in such a way, and carefully walked Sean back through the events on the playground so that he would see that his beef was not with David, but with the children who were teasing the two of them. We also of course emphasized the importance of alternatives to violence. I was burning with rage, thinking to myself that the teacher who had witnessed the fight must have *loved* it—evidence of the soundness of her views about black boys. This same teacher once told a black friend of mine whose daughter was in her class that the school needed more of the "right kind" of black children. The "right kind" of black children are apparently docile, quiet, and female.

When I met with Sean's teacher and an administrator two years ago to discuss a number of issues, I brought up the "David Two/Sean Two" incident, the Noah episode, and others in Sean's school experience, to illustrate the problems of systemic racism that operates even among children. I had to couch this criticism in very careful terms, reiterating several times that I was *not* saying a particular child was racist (indeed, I'm not convinced children can be considered racist), nor was I saying the teacher was racist. I tried to point out how soul-destroying these experiences could be if the child-target met with no support from adults in the school. Black children who are targets of racism may start to doubt the evidence of their own senses and to internalize negative attitudes toward their race when their view of reality is repeatedly dismissed by those in authority.

Actually, I think that this is exactly what black children are supposed to do; that is, the schools teach children a version of Derrick Bell's second rule of racial standing, which goes like this: "Not only are blacks' complaints discounted, but black victims of racism are less effective witnesses than are whites, who are members of the oppressor class. This phenomenon reflects a widespread assumption that blacks, unlike whites, cannot be objective on racial issues and will favor their own no matter what."[14] The least credible (to whites) testimony on race, then, comes from blacks, who are not acknowledged as experts even on their own experience.

A case in point: during that same meeting with the teacher and administrator, I mentioned that several parents had told me of their children's complaints that black children in the school seemed to draw harsher punishments than whites for the same infractions. The teacher instantly dismissed this claim, saying that it was just that black children noticed what happened to black children more than what happened to whites. When I pointed out that one of the children who had observed this discrepancy in punishment was a white girl, the teacher retorted that *of course* this child would have a skewed perspective, because her aunt was a civil rights attorney and they discussed injustice a lot at home. This all suggests an addendum to Bell's second rule of racial standing: whites involved in some way with black struggles are as ineffective witnesses as blacks. I have experienced this rule in action on many occasions, and have internalized it so that I frequently do not reveal my husband's and children's race in discussion of racial issues with whites because I know that if they know about my home life, they will see me as less credible than a white person who does not know any blacks.

A WHITE PARENT ONCE agreed with me that racism was a serious problem in Sean's school, and went on to say that it was part of a widespread lack of good manners. It turns out her daughter is sometimes mocked for her fatness. Well, I'm sure that hurts, but I don't think that sort of teasing is exactly the same as racism, nor do I think racism is a "manners" issue. Douglas Bates reports a similar response from a school administrator, who warned him not to be too sensitive about the racial harassment his daughter was enduring because "all children experience razzing at some point in their lives . . . whether it's for being fat or skinny or having freckles or curly hair."[15] Bates rejected this attempt to put racial insults into the same category as common childhood teasing, but was not able to convince the principal to rethink his views. The authors of *The Color Complex* note that "taunts about color may seem the same as calling a child with glasses 'four eyes' or a fat child 'tubby'—part of the inevitable cruelties of childhood. Yet children can never outgrow skin color as they do other childhood traits."[16] This analysis misses the point, as the key issue is not mutability but power.

One teacher at Sean's school told another—who then told me—that I take racism "too seriously." After all, she went on to say, she was sometimes teased for being Italian in a predominantly Irish neighborhood as a child. Again, I'm sure this hurt—I was often teased for being tall as a child, and it *did* hurt—but it does not have the same implications or effects as racism. This seems self-evident to me, and to every black and antiracist white person I know, yet is a major area of contention among whites generally.

There is a crucial distinction between prejudicial attitudes or biases on the one hand, and racism on the other, particularly institutional or systemic racism. We all have biases or prejudices, ranging from the harmless (I can't bear heavy metal music, for instance) to the hurtful (mocking someone's ethnicity or appearance). Racism differs substantially from these biases in its power to affect its targets' life chances—where one lives, where one works, what sort of job one has, where (or if) one goes to school, what one thinks of oneself and of one's group. Biases against rock music or Italians are not encoded into every social institution, after all, while racism is. School is the first place where children experience systemic racism first-hand, with the lessons coming from the curriculum, the faculty, and the student body.[17]

Andrew Hacker, describing institutional racism in *Two Nations*, asserts that most organizational cultures in the United States—from the FBI to private industry—are "inherently white."[18]

American institutions begin with an initial bias against black applicants, since the presumption is that most blacks cannot or will not meet the standards the organization has set. Historically, virtually all of the people associated with Yale University, United Airlines, and the Omaha police force [to give an arbitrary selection of illustrations] have been white, which has in turn created both the image of these institutions and the way they operate. In this sense, they are "white" organizations, from which it follows that their members are expected to think and act in white ways. This is not as difficult for white people, although some have to make an extra effort if they wish to master class-based aspects of the manner and style. However, for blacks the situation is qualitatively different, since they see themselves as being judged by more coercive criteria, which call on them to deny large parts of themselves.[19]

Institutions are made up of human beings, in a symbiotic relation: the institution conveys its values to individuals, individuals further reinforce (or, less usually, challenge) these values, the institution reflects these attitudes back, and so on. A lifetime of experiences with institutional racism explains why many black parents immediately assume that their children's school difficulties are rooted in racism and treat schools as inherently antagonistic to their children, attitudes that apparently baffle white teachers and administrators.[20] Some schools and businesses are now trying to overcome their institutionalized racism with the help of diversity consultants, but to do so they must battle not only that racism but also the cynical mockery of those who think systemic racism is a chimera.[21]

Systemic racism is no chimera: when Noah told Sean he would not go to college, Noah was expressing an *institutional* bias that he had already internalized at age eight; when my acquaintance's daughter was called "fatty" by a classmate, the classmate was expressing a prejudice, but not one backed up by the full force of social institutions. And that, I think, is the crucial difference—one that is understood by virtually all black people, but surprisingly few whites.

When whites encounter black biases against whites, they tend to label these attitudes "racist" or "reverse racist," but in reality they are nothing of the kind. Black people do not control social institutions, do not have the power to encode their biases into legal and social strictures as whites do. So, while such prejudice is reprehensible and even hurtful to individual white people, it does not have the force of racism. Racism is more than individually held biases. As Andrew Hacker comments, "Racism takes its full form only when it has an impact on the real world. . . . The significance of racism lies in the way it consigns certain human beings to the margins of society, if not painful lives and early deaths. In the United States, racism takes its highest toll on blacks. No white person can claim to have suffered in such ways because of ideas that may be held about them by some black citizens."[22]

THE CUMULATIVE EFFECTS OF dealing with subtle, institutional racism include both exhaustion and paranoia. As my friend Elizabeth recently told me, she used to be committed to integration and to raising her children in as integrated an area as possible, but:

I've come full circle now to the point where I wish to God, with all my heart, that there was an all-black school with an all-black faculty that I could send my children to. . . . So, I'd *know* that if they [the school faculty] called me about something, that would be what was going on: it's her academics, it's her behavior, whatever. I don't want any hidden agendas. . . . I want my child safe, I'm tired of her being hurt and of worrying about the possibility of her being hurt.

For me, the really heartbreaking aspect of Elizabeth's comment is not that she's given up on integration, but that her vision of an all-black institution, free of racism, is purely fantasy. There are, of course, all-black institutions, but I doubt that any are free of racism. Where would these black faculty, administrators, and staff come from? From this society, where they would most certainly have come into contact with *some* nonblack institutions and would in all likelihood have internalized at least some of the institutional racism they encountered. Alice Walker's depiction in *Meridian* of "Saxon College," a black institution that is dedicated to teaching black women to be white ladies and that fences out most of the black community, is illustrative here. In other words, there is no safe place, no pure person: we have all, black or not, been indoctrinated into our society's racist values long before we reach adulthood.

In contrast to my friend Elizabeth's fervent desire for an all-black environment for her child stands my sister-in-law Beverly's advice to Doug and me. When we told her we were planning to move Sean to a school with more black students, Beverly expressed concern. A school principal herself, Beverly felt that the academic preparation Sean received at his first school was truly excellent and wanted to be sure we based our decision on academic as well as racial factors. I realized that we had spoken only about race, as if numbers were the only issue, and reassured her that the new school was, if anything, more academically rigorous than Sean's former school. Beverly still thought we might be making a mistake. "The truth is that Sean has to survive in a racist society. Trying to protect him from racism now could backfire later when he has to deal with racist whites and lacks the tools to do that. I know you want him to be safe, but keeping him safe now could just increase the danger for him later." Beverly's view—that racism is an intrinsic part of our society and that black children are best served by learning to deal with it early—would be alien to the mass of whites.

White people, perhaps trying to demonstrate their own lack of racism, frequently assert that children do not notice race.[23] At the same time, the old saw that you have to be taught to hate seems to have been updated and simplified to mean that your parents have to teach you to hate. This readiness to locate the learning of racism in the home mirrors our society's bourgeois individualism, but it also bespeaks both an unwillingness to acknowledge the *social* nature of racism and a flight from collective responsibility. If racism is as much a part of our culture as baseball, as much a part of the school curriculum as reading, and therefore parents need not teach their children racist ideas, then no one can escape it—we are all implicated. Most white people try to avoid this guilty knowledge.

What would it mean for white people to acknowledge the social nature of racism? Most obviously, it would mean needing to *do* something or to fall victim to a useless, guilt-induced paralysis. And this doing is daunting. Black people tend to identify with other black people victimized in bias incidents—they can see themselves as vulnerable to that harassment, and many have endured similar kinds of harassment. White people—except gays and lesbians—tend to stand outside, identifying neither with the harassed nor with the harassers. This outsider stance speaks powerfully to the effects of white supremacism, as even

women, working or lower class, first-generation college attend-
ers, the children or grandchildren of immigrants, single mothers,
Jews, and feminists share the single privilege of skin color. Most
white people have been indoctrinated into identification with the
upper-class white elites who oppress them too. As bell hooks has
pointed out, in our society all whites are bonded together through
white supremacy.[24]

I am not saying that an antiracist society is unachievable, nor
am I saying that it is hopeless for individual whites to try to
change themselves and the wider society. What I am saying is
that it is hard, very hard. Furthermore, individual change is not
enough—to combat institutional racism, we need cooperative
efforts. And this, I think, is the sticking point. The fact is that
for white people to fight institutional racism and its concomi-
tant white skin privilege, we will have to give something up: we
will have to refuse the unearned privileges accorded us for our
white skins. Apart from the initial problem of raising consciousness enough to recognize these privileges, we will run into the
problem of not wanting to lose our privileges, especially our
(white) children's privileges.

When my son's former school was working on its admissions
policy, the multicultural parents' group offered advice to the
principal on allocating the limited number of places open each
year. To meet the school's affirmative action goals, *all* open
places should be earmarked for minority students, which is what
our group at first advocated. It soon became clear, however, that
white parents' younger children would not be admitted to the
school under such a policy, and our coalition fell apart. Most of
the white parents—all of whom thought of themselves as extremely liberal, if not downright radical—wanted to retain the
old "sibling policy," by which siblings of enrolled children got
preference for admissions. This policy favored white children, as
the vast majority of children already enrolled were white and

therefore their younger siblings, who got preference under this arrangement, were also white. The white parents did not see this as preferential treatment or as favoritism toward whites—which it blatantly was—but *did* see an affirmative action policy as preferential treatment and favoritism toward blacks. During our meeting with the principal, it became clear that these white parents—who were a tiny minority of white parents in the school and who had worked hard in other ways for more diversity—only supported social justice if their own children did not have to forgo their inherited privileges. Furthermore, they did not want *any* white children to lose these privileges, a wish they disguised under concern for the "public relations" of our group: we need to go slowly so as not to alienate other parents.

I believe this episode is a microcosmic example of wider social attitudes. Most white liberals are willing to "add in" blacks, but many are *not* willing to step aside in order to stand next to blacks, are not willing to give up any portion of their own advantages in order to redistribute resources and power more equitably.

WHITES ARE SO UNUSED TO blacks' being treated fairly that they often perceive blacks as getting preferential treatment when they are treated equally. Several years ago I taught a course on narratives of slavery that drew a more diverse group of students than is common at my college. One white student was late for ten of fourteen class meetings, according to my grade book. When she arrived, she would walk across the front of the class, settle herself noisily into a seat, and ask people around her what we were talking about. This was quite disruptive, and I spoke to the student privately on several occasions about the problem. A black student was late three times, and always called me before class when he was going to be late. When he arrived, he would slip into the classroom quietly, taking a seat near the door. The sixth time the white student performed her late arrival/big entrance act, disrupting an intense discussion of *Jubilee*, I snapped, "Would you *please* try to arrive on time?"

On the final evaluations for the course, one student—I assume the often-tardy woman—wrote, "This professor really favors black students. When white students are late, she yells at them, but when black students are late, she's nice to them or doesn't say anything." This comment brought me up short—perhaps I *do* unconsciously favor black students? I mentioned my concern to a colleague, who said, "So what if you do? You'd be the only teacher most of the black students would ever encounter who treated them well, while the white students will have *many* teachers who favor them. Think of it as evening things up." On reflection, though, I think I am not biased in black students' favor. I think I treat black students fairly, that's all; sadly, equitable treatment may be so unusual that it seems like favoritism.

One black student in another class wrote me a note of thanks after the final exam, saying I was the only professor that term who had treated her as "an individual human" and allowed her to express her point of view during class discussions "without either cutting me off or expecting me to speak for all black people." She ended with, "Thanks for redeeming my faith in the basic decency of people—even white people!"

The evaluations for this course—an African and African-American Studies course in which I had focused on revolutionary movements—were superficially glowing, but as I read them I got a picture of myself that made me squirm. All the students had circled "excellent" for every question about the material, my knowledge of the subject, and my overall handling of the course. The comments, on the other hand, depicted someone I did not want to be.

The comment that follows is the one that troubled me most: "Being a white female, she conveys the material in a way that is comfortable to the class. She lets each person state their own opinions and although she may disagree, she does not put down that person's opinion. She also tries not to deal with the emotional aspects of this course." This student's first sentence suggests that I had a special authority in teaching an African/African-American Studies course because I am *not black* (back to Bell's second rule of racial standing) and that I did not cause discomfort in the class. The second sentence does not bother me, but the third sentence, saying that I avoided the "emotional aspects" of the course, I read as damning. After the momentary elation of an unusual number of notes of thanks and an entirely "excellent" quantifiable rating on the evaluations, I was devastated as I realized how seriously I had failed in that course. For one thing, I had somehow managed not to make clear enough my *limitations* as a white person teaching this course. For another, not much learning could have gone on if students really did feel "comfortable," no matter how much they enthused about what they had learned. Finally, race is and ought to be, in this racist society, an emotional topic, and yet I had "avoided" these emotions. I read those evaluations over and over, wondering where I had gone wrong.

I was not going to waste the opportunities the evaluations offered to reconsider my teaching and to make some changes. I think that the "avoided emotions" comment was accurate, and I believe that I created that impression by my zeal to have students take the literature we read seriously and to apply their best intellectual capabilities to analyzing it: I fell into the reason *or* feeling trap. Further, I was concerned about the potential volatility of the material in the context of a racially diverse class of students. In particular, I was trying—wrongly, I now see—to avoid a possible blow-up along racial lines over some predictably foolish comment by one of the white students, as frequently happens in such courses. I kept the lid on too tight: students need to be able to blow up if provoked, and suppressing anger inhibits learning. I was also trying hard to keep my private life out of the course, which was ridiculous: our "private" lives are also political, and they *belonged* in the course. Worst of all, I had not recognized the extent of the authority that my white skin and my academic position gave me in the eyes of my students, and had failed to address that issue of authority, and its limitations, directly.

I would like to say that I have solved these problems, but I have not. I have worked on them, and now believe that the process of working on them will be life-long (or at least, career-long) and that no solution will be either adequate or permanent. In the process of that working, I have used everything I could learn from Sean's experiences in school to interrogate my own teaching. I have also remembered, in every class that I teach, that the idea is to disrupt students' complacency (and my own), to make them (and me) uncomfortable, to encourage us all to use both feeling and intellect to learn and to grow.

6
Mothers,
Daughters,
Sisters,
Comrades

S
PRING, 1992.

As the academic year draws toward a close, Sean frequently expresses relief that summer is coming and that he won't have to deal with "racial stuff" for a few months. Los Angeles is burning three thousand miles away, but racial tensions are running so high everywhere that I feel those flames licking at our door. Ailis is just six months old, happily oblivious to anything outside her immediate sensory range, where things are close to perfect. On the days that I teach, my parents take care of Ailis; my mother in particular seems convinced that Ailis is not only the most beautiful girl in the world, but also the smartest. I think Ailis is a genius, she tells me seriously several times a week; just listen to what she did today.

My friend Karen's sorority schedules an evening of entertainment to kick off their annual conference, and Karen invites me to be her guest. Well aware of the historical importance of black sororities and curious about how these sororities work now, I am delighted to be invited. After I get the particulars of time and place and accept the invitation, Karen adds, "You'll probably be the only white person there." I say the first thing that comes to mind, "That's okay—it won't be the first time, and I'm sure you've been the only black person at many events."

Something in Karen's expression and the way she pats my arm clues me in: this was a test, and I passed. My pleasure at being invited to her sorority's conference is now tempered by sorrowful anger that Karen still feels she has to test me three years into our friendship. Still, I remind myself that our friendship exists within a cultural and historical context whose every particular tells Karen, a black woman, that she should not trust white women, and I am a white woman. Our friendship is a triumph of individual personalities over historical conditions, as are all friendships between women across the color line, with Karen risking more than I. I should not be surprised at being tested. Nevertheless, it hurts, as does every such reminder that race remains a barrier.

Several weeks later, with the sorry history of relationships between black and white women much on my mind, I arrive at the conference hotel, where Karen greets me with pleasure, and whispers, "Now I can get Henry [her husband] to leave the bar and come in here, 'cause he has you to sit with." Karen once told me that Henry deeply mistrusts and dislikes white people in general, and tries to avoid any dealings with whites. I am one of his few exceptions because, in Karen's words, "You have a black husband and black children, so he thinks you can be friends."

As Henry and I take our seats at a table with six sorority members—Karen must sit on a dais with the other officers—I find grim humor in the irony that the same black husband and children that signify my acceptability to Henry would surely mean something quite different to the women at the table. I decide not to "come out," and hope Henry doesn't say anything that would reveal my husband's race. The sorority members make me welcome as Karen's friend, and the evening turns out to be great fun, with interesting speeches, lively musical and dance performances by young sorority and fraternity members, and stimulating conversation at our table. It is a great break from the stress I've been experiencing all week, but I feel like an imposter through all this, not entitled to the warm hospitality extended by women who might not want to be such gracious hosts if they knew about my family. Or, more honestly, my husband.

Toward the end of the evening, I discover that I have misread the situation. A sorority member who worked at Sean's old day-care center comes to sit at our table and asks me how Sean is doing in school. Turning to the other women at the table, Donna says, "Her son was a beautiful child, and *sweet*! He's going to be a heartbreaker. We'll see him on the cover of *Ebony* some day." No one blinks an eye. One of the women says to me, "While you were up getting a drink, Henry was telling us that your boy is getting a hard time from some of the white kids in his class and you're not too happy with his school. I had the same complaints when my daughter was at that school." As everyone at the table joins into a conversation about how the schools fail black children, I am chagrined to realize that while imagining I was in a racial closet, I have actually been "out" all the time. And I have foolishly misjudged my hosts. Through my misjudgment, I have missed an opportunity to connect with black women on more than a superficial level.

In an earlier chapter, I mentioned the problem of racial standing in "coming out" to people as the white mother of black children. I hesitate with blacks and whites for different reasons: whites because I worry that knowledge of my personal life will cause them to discount what I say about race, and blacks, especially women, because I worry that coming out will diminish the possibility of connection.[1]

I have encountered enough minor variations on these responses to make me wary. For instance, about halfway through a women's studies course I taught a few years ago, I mentioned during a discussion of race and color that my children are black. It seemed dishonest not to acknowledge my own stake in a debate that had become quite personal for many of my students. Some black students came to my office later to tell me this revelation had been a mistake. It seems that a group of white students discussed my comment after class, with general agreement that my personal life explained why the course included what they saw as too much attention to black women's writing. As one student later put it on the course evaluation, "I don't think we should have to read so much stuff about race. The course is supposed to be about *women* and *women's problems*. The readings about race just take our attention away from the real problems, like abortion and sexual harassment." Despite months of reading and classroom discussion, this student evidently still believed that "woman" means "white," and that race fell outside the category of "real problem." In this case my revelation did not harm my relations with black women students, perhaps because they were angered by the white students' response and saw me as an ally in this situation.

For black men—regardless of their attitude toward interracial marriages—my marriage and children seem to signal that I am not one of "them," that I am probably not getting ready to call the police because they glanced in my direction. On the other hand, my marriage may pose an additional barrier to the already slim possibility of friendly connection with black women. Too often, I have met a black woman, hit it off with her, and then seen our nascent friendship freeze as soon as she met or heard about Doug. Additionally, I've read numerous accounts by black women of their anger at white women who marry across the color line, and I have had friends and acquaintances tell me forthrightly that they have or had a serious problem with cross-racial marriages in general.

Sometimes a black woman will indicate that she knows everything she needs to know about me, and more than she wanted to, when she discovers I have a black husband. Once, a few weeks into a course on African-American literature that I was teaching, a black woman student stopped by my office to ask about an assignment. Pointing at the picture of my son on my desk, she asked, "Is that your child?" When I acknowledged he was, she said "Ohhh," in a tone that seemed to me to carry the whole terrible tale of black and white women's relationships.

Looking back, I see that Lena's "ohhh" constituted a defining moment for me, as it came at an important time of convergence in my life. I was teaching African-American literature, and on the day that Lena first came to talk with me we had begun discussing Harriet Jacobs's *Incidents in the Life of a Slave Girl*. Jacobs addresses her narrative to the "mothers of America" and at several points speaks directly to white women as mothers, calling for their sympathy and demanding that they act maternally to end slavery. My students had focused their comments on the vicious white mistress who blamed Jacobs herself for her own husband's sexual assaults on the "slave girl."

At the same time, I was helping to organize parents of "minority" children at my son's school, which involved forming alliances with black women, many of whom initially viewed me with suspicion. I was also working on an article about portrayals of motherhood in fiction by both black and white women. As director of my college's women's studies program, I was trying to figure out how to attract more women of color, both students and faculty, to that program. How could we in women's studies design a better, truly multiracial program? As chair of a college committee on race relations, I was hearing many complaints from black women about their marginalization on campus.

As has happened so often with me, I was feeling real dissonance between my "public" life and my life within my family. Inside my family, I never felt race as a barrier between women, never experienced the kind of racial tension that was so central a topic in other parts of my life. From very early in Doug's and my relationship, the women in his family opened their hearts to me. My mother-in-law, Marguerite, has been a second mother to me for so many years now that I quite literally cannot imagine not having her in my life, and have real trouble remembering a time when she was not an important part of my life. Doug's sister, Beverly, and I are very close as well, and Doug believes that I brought the two of them closer together. One of Doug's aunts, Ricky, has been more influential in my life than any of my own aunts or uncles. With marriage to Doug, I got the extended family I never before had, and the women of Doug's family have always been the most important elements of that family. I took the good will and sincerity of my relatives by marriage for granted, as they took mine, and so we started from assumptions precisely the opposite of those that govern most encounters between black and white women. And these assumptions made the path to loving acceptance smooth.

Finally, I was pregnant and knew that my child would be a girl. Having Lena—a student I liked, who made insightful comments in class and wrote a terrific first paper—dismiss any possibility of connection with a single syllable when she discovered my son's race moved me to try to bring all of these elements of my life together, to do *something* to improve relations between black and white women. But what? How can we learn to trust each other and to work together in our mutual interests? And what are our mutual interests?

I am certain that silence about race matters is not in our mutual interest, tempting as it may be since speech is fraught with fears and difficulties. As Audre Lorde once pointed out, however, it is not really our differences that divide women from each other, but our silence, our unwillingness to risk speaking honestly about those differences.[2] Although I think that more than silence divides black and white women from each other, I also believe that silence widens that divide and makes it seem dauntingly unbridgeable even to black and white women who want to construct a multiracial feminist movement.

Black and white women's overlapping but divergent histories in this country and the highly sexualized nature of racism together create chasms of misunderstanding between us. As a feminist, I have long been deeply concerned about relationships between black and white women; this concern has gained greater urgency for me since the birth of my daughter, Ailis, a black girl who will be raised to womanhood by a white mother. My concern, then, is both political and profoundly personal, in multiple, converging ways. The point at which the personal and the political daily interconnect is in my work as a teacher, where I struggle to help my students find common ground on which we can speak.

At this historical moment, in which we see backsliding in rights for blacks of both genders and for women of all races, and a backlash against all manner of civil rights, the absolute necessity of working together hardly needs explanation. And yet . . . we—black and white women—have made little progress toward forming coalitions, much less establishing friendships. We seem trapped in history, mired in mutual misunderstanding.

Both black and white feminists in the United States generally acknowledge an urgent need for white women to educate ourselves about black women if the feminist movement is to progress, or even to survive. I agree, but I also believe that black women need to educate themselves about white feminist realities as well. While white women in general are treated scornfully in much black women's theoretical writing, white feminists are demonized, treated precisely as we are accused of treating black women.[3] Black women writers who identify themselves as feminist, such as bell hooks, and who work for cross-racial alliances among women report sharp criticisms from other black women and see their own work marginalized or even trashed.

Reading feminist theory by both black and white women might lead one to conclude that a multiracial feminist movement is unachievable, that it is a hopeless endeavor. That is certainly what many of my women's studies students took away from their reading for my class last fall, although it is not what I expected to teach. At the same time, increasing numbers of young black and white women see feminism as irrelevant to their lives and, in poll after poll, assert that they are not feminist. Although surveys usually show greater support for fundamental feminist concerns—pay equity, social equality of men and women, child-care support, and the like—among black women than among white, black women are less likely than whites to identify themselves as feminists, to choose that label. Alice Walker's famous invention of "womanist" (as a more congenial description for black women than "feminist" because the former is rooted in black culture while the latter presumably is not) reflects widely shared attitudes toward feminism as a middle-class white women's movement.

My friend Karen, who not only is active in a black sorority but also willingly serves as a personal and professional mentor to large numbers of young black women—who, in other words, consistently acts on what I think of as feminist attitudes and beliefs—surprised me once by asserting that she is not a feminist. Her explanation was that she is uncomfortable with what she sees as man-bashing among white feminists. Karen's comments find echoes in comments by other black women I know, who speak of their divided loyalties, a division that many believe is not understood or respected by most white feminists.[4] But some white feminists *do* understand and respect black women's position, a fact which too often is ignored by black feminists. White feminists are not all the same, just as not all black feminists are the same, and being treated as identical to one another and especially as identical to white nonfeminists also stands in the way of a multiracial feminist movement.

T H E   N O T I O N   O F   S I S T E R H O O D itself, the philosophic cornerstone of feminism, is fraught with racial traps. Sisterhood has very particular church-based and civil rights movement–based meanings and resonances among black women. Black sororities historically have built on sisterhood as a basis for political action, which may be one source of white feminists' use of the term. As Maria Lugones points out, white feminist appropriation of the sororal model for women's relationships ignored these meanings, along with other grave problems with sisterhood as a political model, setting the stage two decades ago for the racial divide we see in feminism today.[5]

Feminism needs to be revitalized, not buried. I am not willing to abandon feminism's promise for *all* women, hopeless as things may now look, but I do think we need a new political coalition structured on something other than a sororal model. And we need to put our differences to use for all of us.

Furthermore, interracial relationships between women in feminist groups and in feminist writings generally seem far worse than they appear in my own life. My personal experience is not often mirrored in feminist theory, which leads me to conclude that perhaps circumstances are not quite as dire between black and white women as that theory would suggest. At the risk of sounding like the stereotypical white liberal, I must say that I have a number of close black women friends, as well as a very large circle of black women colleagues and acquaintances with whom I work on various political issues, ranging from electoral politics to school curricula.

One common thread in these relationships is that all began with some point of mutual interest and slowly grew from there, in the case of friendships, or remained focused on one issue or cluster of issues, in the case of political alliances. That point of mutual interest has often been black children, a theme that I see repeated frequently in my life and in black women's imaginative literature.

Despite all the things that divide us, one area in which black and white women sometimes seem able to form coalitions for working together is that concerning children, our own and others. This suggests to me that although the sororal model of feminism may not be workable across racial lines, an "othermother" model, to use Patricia Hill Collins's term designating women who care for children not their own by blood or legal adoption, might be more fruitful.[6] Black women have often reached out to my children through me or to me through my children.

A black woman administrator at a college where I once worked took one look at Sean on the first day we visited the campus and made a beeline for us across a crowded courtyard. She soon discovered I was having trouble finding good child care in the area. A few minutes after excusing herself to make a phone call, this woman—whom we had known for under an hour—came back with a slip of paper. The phone call had been to a friend of hers, also black and a fellow alumna of a historically black college, who directed a program we had heard about but had been told was full. There was space for Sean after this call. Our new friend said to me, "When you called, Jeannie didn't know you were calling about a *black* boy—she's always looking out for black kids to enroll in the center."

When I first met Doug's mother, sister, and aunt, I was struck by the many different ways in which they acted on what I saw as political commitments, although no one expressed these commitments in explicitly political terms. Doug's sister, Beverly, for instance, who was then a teacher, was making a dress for a former student to wear to her eighth-grade graduation. Beverly's reasoning was that otherwise this child, whose family was poor, would not have a special dress for an occasion Beverly hoped she would celebrate. "This is a really smart girl," Bev told me, "and I want her to be proud of herself. She won't feel good getting up there to give her speech if she doesn't *look* good, so . . ."

This private act of kindness had a political dimension, I believe, as does all such "othermothering": by committing herself to a particular child (or children) for reasons other than bourgeois individualism, a woman commits herself to the future and strikes a blow against a social system that tries to push us all into rigidly bounded nuclear families that compete against each other for ever scarcer rewards.[7] As a feminist, I think that any actions that undermine oppressive family and political structures are probably good for women in the aggregate, which is one reason the "othermother model" appeals to me.

Another reason for its appeal is that my own route to feminism began with my mother, and with what my mother told me about her childhood. Although I came of age at a time when feminism among white women could be seen largely as daughters' critiques of mothers' alliances with patriarchy, I never experienced feminism as that daughter's critique.[8] I saw the feminist movement as a public, politicized version of the ideals I had learned from my mother. I became a feminist in part because I loved my mother, and the feminist movement seemed to offer an arena for action in honor of that love. From the beginning, I perceived feminism as a movement for social change, not about life-styles but about politics, and specifically about collective political action to improve *all* women's lives.[9]

Although my mother is Irish, not African-American, her personal history corresponds closely with the patterns Collins identifies as typical of African-American communities. Given away when she was three days old by parents who never explained why they did not want her and who went on to have eight children they kept, my mother was raised by an elderly couple she always called Mammy and Daddy, although they did not formally adopt her. When this couple died, my mother was fourteen, and other women she knew—all achingly poor—took her to live with them for various periods of time. My mother's attitude toward her childhood, and her great love for the women who gave her a home, along with her own extensive "othermothering" activities, contributed to my developing an empathy for my mother that Gloria Joseph sees as more common among black daughters than among whites. Like the black daughters Joseph describes in her sections of *Common Differences*, I understood early my mother's limited power in the world and saw her as my ally, not as my enemy. In getting to know my mother-in-law and sister-in-law, I found a continuity with my relationship with my mother and with my deepest political commitments. Although personal and political relationships are not necessarily coterminous, I think their trajectories intersect at a point that I would call love. The "othermother" model of interracial relationships among women acknowledges the necessity of love.

Because of my professional training and my long-standing predilections, I am in the habit of turning to imaginative literature for insight when thinking through difficult issues. Several novels by black women support the idea that connecting as "othermothers" may lead to cross-racial alliances and even friendships. These novels—Toni Morrison's *Beloved*, Alice Walker's *Meridian*, and Sherley Anne Williams's *Dessa Rose*—depict highly symbolic versions of joint work on mothering and on other specific issues. The striking consistency of elements in the novels' temporary, child-centered relationships between black and white women characters suggests shared attitudes toward the conditions under which an interracial feminist movement might be possible.

Imaginative literature by black women offers white women a kind of access to black women's thought not readily gained elsewhere. Collins argues that black women's thought is rooted in what I would call a practicalist conception of truth, with practicalism holding that particular practices give rise to distinctive ways of thinking. Collins points to the widespread conviction among African-American women that "what one does and how one thinks" are causally connected.[10] I have argued elsewhere that attentive reading may offer access to forms of thought arising from practices different from a reader's own, just as a literary scholar can learn how scientific thought works.[11] Thus, although white women can never live black women's lives in a racist society, and therefore cannot engage in many of the practices that structure black women's thought, white women *can* learn how that thought works, can attend to the practices from which it arises, and can take account of it in our own ways of thinking. One of the many dangers raised for white feminists by the project of attentive reading from a self-consciously raced and gendered position is the objectification of black women as figures of authority.[12] I recognize that black women writers and black feminists are not monolithic in their views, a recognition that I hope will help me to avoid that trap, while still noting points of similarity in these novels.

Beloved, Meridian, and *Dessa Rose* all show white women as blind to the actual conditions of black people's lives, and therefore ignorant of the political structure within which they themselves live.[13] Worse yet, their blindness and ignorance are often willful. These women characters are adults, and as such have no right to refuse to know about the world around them. Their ignorance is not innocent, but morally and ethically reprehensible. Both *Dessa Rose* and *Beloved*, for instance, show comparatively kindly white women unquestioningly accepting the institution of slavery, perceiving it either as a natural phenomenon or as a man-made system with which they have little to do. The failure of these white women to question slavery makes possible the outrages the novels dramatize. *Meridian*, set a century after the abolition of slavery, describes a similar blindness in Lynne, who sees black people as essentially without agency—as objects to be pitied or to be admired as Art.

Initially, none of the white female characters in these three novels has any sense of a common bond between women across the divide of race, even of a bond based on a sense of shared gender victimization. Significantly, the black women characters also at first fail to see parallels between their condition and that of the white women. Morrison's Sethe first recognizes some common ground during the birth of her daughter, when she is helped by a white girl, Amy Denver. Amy sees Sethe's lacerated back and exclaims, "What God have in mind, I wonder. I had me some whippings, but I don't remember nothing like this. Mr. Buddy had a right evil hand too. . . . [Once] he hauled off and threw the poker at me."[14] Despite this acknowledgment that she and Sethe can both be beaten by white men and her later mention of her mother's being "give to Mr. Buddy" as an indentured servant and therefore probably also as a sexual object, Amy insists rather on her difference from Sethe, repeatedly claiming that Sethe "don't know a thing" and that she, Amy, does.[15] Sethe, however, realizes that they are both runaways, "two throw-away people, two lawless outlaws."[16] Naming her child "Denver" is Sethe's acknowledgment of a link with the "whitegirl," as Morrison renders the description throughout *Beloved*.

Similarly, Dessa and Meridian at first fail to imagine common ground with white women. Sick and disoriented, Dessa first thinks Rufel, the white woman, is a dream apparition and that she symbolizes "your enemies" or "death."[17] Once she realizes that Rufel is real, Dessa still refuses to *think* of her as real and tries to block out Rufel's words: "She knew she could understand what the white woman said if she would let herself. But if she understood the white woman, she would have to . . . have to, have to do—Something."[18]

White people "did not seem quite real" to Meridian,[19] and white women seem especially unreal: "white women were considered sexless, contemptible and ridiculous by all. . . . They were clear, dead water."[20] Unlike black women, who are "outrageous," white women grow up only to sink "into a permanent oblivion. One never heard of them *doing* anything that was interesting."[21] There are multiple contradictions here: for one thing, Meridian's thoughts do not correspond to what we are *shown* in *Meridian*, where we do not see any black women being "outrageous," except perhaps Meridian herself. Further, although white women are considered "contemptible by all," white womanhood is also adopted as a (destructive) model by several black women, including Meridian's own mother, and is the tacit model for the "ladyhood" into which students are supposed to be indoctrinated at all-black Saxon College.

I think that what's going on here, in the characters of Meridian and Dessa, is a struggle to come to terms with white women's paradoxical power and powerlessness. Each character wants to cast white women as the Other, to define herself *against* white women, and yet knows on some level that black and white women share certain problems. Recognizing the shared elements of oppression would require doing "something," to quote Dessa, but figuring out what that something might be remains confusing and painful.

In a pattern that critic Elizabeth Abel identifies as having "dominated black women's narrative representations of women's fraught connections across racial lines,"[22] the relationships between black and white women characters in these three novels are mediated by men. Morrison multiply triangulates the Sethe-Amy dyad with three men, all absent. Williams and Walker create triangles on a black woman–black man–white woman pattern. In both *Dessa Rose* and *Meridian*, a black woman's relationship with a black man is disrupted by a white woman who swiftly becomes the man's lover. Both Dessa and Meridian are utterly bewildered when black men evince sexual interest in white women. Both characters interpret this interest as a personal betrayal. Dessa says, "White woman was everything I feared and hated, and it hurt me that one of them [black men] would want to love with her."[23] On some level, of course, the interracial sexual relationships in these novels *are* betrayals because they are based largely on race and skin color. Nathan of *Dessa Rose* is drawn to have sex with white women because of the danger,[24] while *Meridian*'s Truman "had wanted a woman perfect in all the eyes of the world,"[25] which meant a white virgin.

The interracial romances Williams and Walker invent conform very closely to stereotypes about black men and white women, with the men depicted as colorstruck and the women as in search of illicit thrills. Williams creates a more finely nuanced portrait than does Walker, and seems willing to imagine that a white woman could grow out of racism through a love that begins in racist myths but that acquires a different dimension over time. Neither Lynne nor Rufel ever tries to understand black women's perception of interracial sexual relationships, an omission that limits their growth. And neither relationship lasts. Rufel (at the end of the novel known by her actual name of Ruth) and Nathan separate at novel's end, with Ruth having come to a better understanding of the meaning of their love.[26]

Lynne does eventually gain some wisdom—after she is raped, after she prostitutes herself, after Truman leaves her, after Camara dies—but she can express her knowledge to Truman only in furious, vengeful words: "You only married me because you were too much of a coward to throw a bomb at all the crackers who make you sick . . . and you wanted something *strange* around the house to entertain your friends."[27]

Meridian and Lynne are eventually able to talk about the racial dimension of their own relationship and others, with Lynne expressing her hard-won understanding to Meridian more positively if more sadly than she does to Truman. Walker's decision to portray Meridian and Lynne as beginning to speak "intimately, like sisters" through their shared experience of the terrible loss of a black child—a loss explicitly linked in the narrative with the racist murders of other black people—finds thematic parallels in Williams's and Morrison's later choices.[28] In *Beloved*, Amy and Sethe work together to deliver Sethe's baby and to preserve the infant's life. In *Dessa Rose*, Rufel nurses Dessa's infant when Dessa's breast milk dries up. A crucial difference between Walker's work, on the one hand, and Morrison's and Williams's, on the other, lies in the fate of the child: Lynne loses her child and Meridian shares that loss, while in the two other novels the women succeed in their efforts to save the child. That is, in *Meridian* the bond is based on tragedy: the white woman must suffer personally the horrifying loss of the child she loves before she can empathize with black women. In *Dessa Rose* and *Beloved*, the children's survival unites black and white women. Furthermore, in both Morrison's and Williams's novels, the white woman also nurses the black woman, while in Walker's novel Meridian needs that nursing, but it is provided finally by a black man, Truman.

Despite these important distinctions, however, in all three novels the only significantly positive connections between black and white women come about because of black children. How-ever temporarily, the women create child-centered relationships based on the shared fact of a broadly defined motherhood: all women's responsibility to protect and to nurture all children. With this reading, the novels encode a vision similar to feminist philosopher Sara Ruddick's conception of a politicized, feminist version of maternal thinking, which Ruddick posits as a possi-ble basis of an antiracist peace politics.[29] Rufel's and Amy's acting as "othermothers" to Dessa's and Sethe's children presents a pattern akin to the structures Patricia Hill Collins describes as typical of African-American communities, while Lynne's per-sonal loss leads to her beginning to develop what Collins calls a "community othermother" consciousness.[30]

Sethe's relationship with Amy ends as soon as Denver is born and swaddled for travel; Amy's role is that of literal and meta-phorical midwife, as her aid helps Sethe give birth both to Denver and to her escape into the North. Rufel's relationships with Dessa and with Mony, Dessa's son, and Lynne's with her child, Camara, and with Meridian are more enduring and more complex. Through mothering and then losing Camara, Lynne gains some insight into black mothers' experiences, which his-torically and at the present moment are always fraught with danger, uncertainty, the threat of loss. As Audre Lorde describes this experience, "Raising Black children—female and male—in the mouth of a racist, sexist, suicidal dragon is perilous and chancy."[31] Lynne's love of Camara and her consequent recogni-tion of the many social forces that work to destroy all black people lead her to refuse the false privilege her whiteness con-fers. She tells Meridian that she is now homeless, that she has no family, because Camara "was my *child*. I'd have to walk over my child's *grave* to go back, and I won't."[32]

When Rufel nurses Dessa's baby, a process of consciousness raising begins that finally brings her to denounce slavery and to do whatever she can, at great personal risk, to end the enslavement of one group of people. When Mony cries with hunger, "Rufel had taken the baby to her bosom almost without thought . . . it had seemed to her as natural as tuneless crooning or baby talk."[33] Later Rufel feels "some mortification at becoming wet nurse for a darky," but soon forgets this feeling "in the wonder she felt at the baby."[34]

In Rufel, Williams creates an especially interesting example of a dynamic that is central in feminist theories of mothering. Feminist theorists have stressed the psychological complexity of the experience of mothering, since mothers are also always, simultaneously, daughters; our experience of mothering inevitably evokes the earlier experience of being mothered, making us particularly vulnerable to the return of childhood fantasies.[35] Rufel is a white woman who was mothered by a black woman, not her birth mother; then, in turn, she mothers a black child who is not her biological child and whose birth mother is herself actively engaged in mothering the child. Rufel recalls that her "Mammy," Dorcas, was the only person who treated her with love and kindness, who made her feel both special and wanted; until she gets to know Dessa, Rufel assumes that Dorcas loved her fully and freely. Her longing for the lost, dead mother, Dorcas, is palpable at certain moments ("Mammy, Mammy's hands in her hair—Sudden longing pierced Rufel"), and the memory of Dorcas is Rufel's guide in most situations.[36] She takes in the escaped slaves and nurses Mony as a way of gaining Dorcas's love even after Dorcas's death, always imagining what Dorcas would say and do and searching for physical similarities between Dorcas and Dessa.[37]

Dessa and Rufel have a ferocious argument over Dorcas when Dessa confuses Rufel's "Mammy" with her own, also dead, mother. In the aftermath of this argument, Rufel realizes that she has never thought about Dorcas as a person, separate from herself.

Belated recognition of boundaries and of the role of slavery in her relationship with Dorcas begins Rufel's growth out of racism. In constructing this process of growth, Williams suggests that the development of white women into antiracists parallels a child's growth into a certain amount of autonomy. The clear implication is that racism stunts white women's psychological development, trapping them in an extended childhood.

Rufel's mothering of Mony is in part an attempt to recapture the closeness she once felt to Dorcas—a closeness her white birth children cannot provide—but it is also a movement toward adulthood, an attempt to give to another what Dorcas once gave her. Much as Lynne's love of Camara leads her to see black people as individual subjects, not amorphous objects, and to reject white skin privilege, Rufel's mothering Mony leads her to see black people as fully human, to think about Dorcas for the first time as a separate person with a unique subjectivity:

> Had Mammy had children, Rufel wondered, suckled a child at her breast as she did with the wench's, as she did with her own? . . . Had Mammy minded when the family no longer called her name? Was that why she changed mine? Rufel thought fearfully. Was what she had always thought loving and cute only revenge, a small reprisal for all they'd taken from her? How old *had* Mammy been? . . . Had she any children?[38]

Of the three novels discussed here, Williams's gives the most extensive attention to the shifts in the thought of both black and white women necessary for interracial understanding. Dessa, too, must learn; she must think of Rufel as a human being, not merely as a white woman, symbolic of "death" or "your enemies." As Rufel begins to overcome her own racism—through nursing Mony, remembering Dorcas, loving Nathan, and spending time with the escaped slaves on the farm—Dessa becomes increasingly uneasy: "where white peoples look at black and see something ugly, something hateful, she saw color. I knowed this but I couldn't understand it and it scared me."[39] Dessa and Rufel work together in a scheme to gain enough money for the black people to move out West and for Rufel to live without her husband. The crucial, barrier-destroying moment in their relationship comes when Dessa helps Rufel fight off a white would-be rapist. Whereas once Dessa had looked at Rufel and seen "white," she now also sees "woman": "The white woman was subject to the same ravishment as me . . . I wasn't zactly warm with her, understand; I didn't know how to be warm with no white woman. But now it was like we had a secret between us . . . she was as helpless in this [white male attack] as I was, that our only protection was ourselfs and each other."[40]

There is still an important gap of wisdom between Dessa and Rufel, since Rufel naively assumes that all white people are like herself and that, as Dessa says, "if white folks knew slaves as she knew us, wouldn't be no slavery."[41] Dessa, of course, knows better: "As far as white folks not knowing how bad slavery was—they the ones made it, was the ones kept it."[42] Eventually, Rufel learns some of what Dessa knows, a knowledge that makes her dislike whites and be unwilling to live around those who accept slavery. Like Lynne, she voluntarily becomes homeless. Despite these changes and their close cooperation in the money scheme, Rufel and Dessa do not speak freely to one another, do not become friends, until Rufel risks her life to preserve Dessa's, lying to a sheriff to get Dessa out of jail. This plot line suggests that for black and white women to establish real relationships, there must be not only mutual recognition of both similarities and differences, but also equivalence of danger, of accepted risk.

Taken together, my readings of *Dessa Rose*, *Meridian*, and

Beloved reveal a basic pattern that might help white feminists to act on behalf of a multiracial feminist movement. First, a white woman recognizes and accepts her personal responsibility to preserve and to protect a black child; put more broadly, a white woman commits herself to *children*, to the future. Through this commitment, she learns about the reality of black women's lives; if she can attend to this reality, as Rufel and Lynne do but Amy does not, she may come to understand the political system within which she herself lives and to which she has implicitly lent her support. This knowledge leads her to repudiate the social privilege conferred by white skin and to cast her lot with black women. Significantly, all three novels strongly imply that it is incumbent upon the white woman to educate *herself*, not to rely upon black women to teach her. She must assume adult responsibility and learn to see herself as a constructive agent in the world. When the white woman accepts this responsibility and begins to act on it, and when the black woman has, in turn, recognized some possible connection with her, then the opportunity for cross-racial friendship opens.

These three novels further point to the revolutionary potential of an interracial female alliance. In their pages, black and white women who make common cause seriously disrupt the status quo, which depends in part on keeping the two separate. Even the fragile, temporary, small alliances established by characters in these novels subvert white patriarchal power: both Amy and Sethe escape their "masters" into the North, while the infant whose birth Amy assists is the only one of Sethe's children *not* born into slavery. Dessa and Rufel similarly escape the South, as do the other escaped slaves, their migration West made possible by money conned from slave owners. Lynne and Meridian (separately) commit themselves to exposing, and to dismantling, the corrupt, death-dealing political system that oppresses them.

The pattern in these novels, however, while undeniably offering some hope for truly inclusive feminist theory and practice, also has other, more troubling implications. These books suggest that we can become sisters only through being mothers, that it is only through mothering that white women can begin to understand and to appreciate black women's thought. Amy, the one white character who does not engage in sustained mothering of a black child and who therefore has the most shallow relationship to a black woman, also exhibits the least change in consciousness. Historically, women's capacity to give birth has been used to oppress us; that capacity has been treated as a necessity, and motherhood has been defined as a central aspect of all women's role. If we can be comrades only if we first are mothers, does supporting an interracial feminism require an implicit endorsement of precisely those attitudes that oppress all women? Does it also exclude women who are not mothers? And does it recapitulate white women's historic relation to objectified black maternal figures of fantasy?

Further, since the two white characters who change the most and who establish the longest-lasting, deepest relationships with black women in these books are sexually and romantically involved with black men, do these novels covertly support sexual relationships between black men and white women, a phenomenon their protagonists directly attack? Alternatively, should we read these novels as saying interracial feminism ultimately is impossible to sustain, as it requires that which is *most* likely to offend and to alienate black women further from white women? And isn't there a serious problem in basing women's relationships with women on our relationships with men? At the end of *Dessa Rose*, Dessa tells us that Nathan and Rufel finally separated, Rufel moving North and Nathan heading West. Although Dessa remembers Rufel fondly, their relationship, too, is effectively severed by distance. When *Meridian* ends, Lynne and Truman remain separate, despite Lynne's wish for a reconciliation. This novel is so open-ended that we do not know what finally happens between Lynne and Meridian, but it seems unlikely that they will sustain the close bond they formed after Camara's death, because Lynne simply is not very important in Meridian's life.

Collins's analysis of black women's thought as rooted in an ethic of care and in the practicalist tenet that what one does influences how one thinks offers another approach to these novels. From this perspective, to understand black women's thought and to integrate it into our own consciousnesses, white women must *do* something beyond reading and theorizing that places us closer to black women's position in society. We can read Rufel's and Lynne's mothering of black children as expressing this doing, as smaller figures for the collective action white women must take if we want to establish relationships with black women. With this reading, Williams and Walker do not necessarily suggest that white women must give birth to black children or otherwise mother them directly. Rather, these novels suggest that white women must attempt to understand black women's experience, and to do so we must renounce white skin privilege and commit ourselves to working for a nonracist future. Whereas white feminists have in the past sometimes arrogated to themselves the right to define the agenda for all feminists, these novels suggest that only by committing ourselves to a politics of liberation—the agenda black feminists have limned—that does not privilege gender over race will we ever be really free. This renunciation of false privilege and serious commitment to a multiracial future— a future in which *all* children, and therefore all people, are valued and protected—will never come about through constructing a sisterhood. Family models are problematic in all kinds of ways, but the one role in the family through which women might form enduring cross-racial alliances is the role of mother.[43] Mothers are committed to preservation and to the future in ways that sisters are not, or at least do not have to be. Hence the "othermother" model may be especially useful.

Another, more explicitly political way to express this co-mothering model of connection among women might be comradeship. Black and white women need to be each other's comrades, a kind of political friendship that recognizes differences and works *because* of them, not in spite of them. Thinking of each other as comrades might keep alive in us all the necessary understanding that comradeship, like friendship, can be withdrawn or lost and requires ongoing care to sustain, unlike sisterhood, which implies an unconditional love that is unrealistic to expect.[44]

The mothering that goes on in *Meridian*, *Dessa Rose*, and *Beloved* also offers white women a model of motherhood rooted in African-American experience, not privatized but cooperative and collective.[45] This model could be used as the basis of comradeship. Perhaps paradoxically, given the need to control motherhood in order to reproduce existing power relations, mothering offers black and white women a way to move beyond connections based on a shared victimization. If black and white American women can begin alliances only by recognizing our shared oppression, we must also recognize that we can effect social change only through strength. In these three novels, mothering provides the opportunity first to acknowledge socially enforced weakness, and then to develop and to capitalize upon mutual strengths.

These strengths are the ones I hope to pass along to my children, and a cross-racial feminist movement—a movement of comrades—offers the best hope that I can see for creating a future in which my children can blossom. The confusion my children inevitably will experience as a result of American racial schizophrenia requires not only personal strength but also politics to sort out. The tools that Doug and I are trying hard to give Sean and Ailis—self-esteem, resistance, independence of mind, critical consciousness, a sense of justice—are of course basic political tools. We also want our children to see themselves as part of a collective enterprise, not as loners on the stage of life.

I talk with friends and relatives, and read everything I can find on race, looking for ideas to help all four of us join in this collective enterprise. Reading Patricia Williams's *The Alchemy of Race and Rights* while I was pregnant with Ailis, I was struck by an analysis that encapsulated both why I can find so little on this topic and why Ailis and I must be not only mother and daughter, but also political allies, comrades. I would like Ailis to be led to feminist politics through love, and I never want her to have to choose between her mother (me) and black women, or to see her allegiance to one as betrayal of the other. Discussing Judge Sorkow's opinion in the so-called Baby M case, legal theorist Williams explores the implications of Sorkow's comment that it is "natural" for people to want children "like" themselves. Interrogating this supposition, Williams turns to racial difference:

> Is there not something unseemly, in our society, about the spectacle of a white woman mothering a black child? A white woman giving totally to a black child; a black child totally and demandingly dependent for everything, sustenance itself, from a white woman. . . . Such a picture says there is no difference; it places the hope of continuous generation, of immortality of the white self, in a little black face.[46]

This spectacle is unseemly even to those operating from a politics of race unlike Sorkow's. A letter to the editor in a recent issue of *Colors* that rails against transracial adoption and all other familial relations between blacks and whites claims that "short of having an African mate, one of the greatest desires of the white woman is to have something no white man can give her: a child of color."[47]

The "unseemliness" of my family translates into invisibility, even in feminist theory that is otherwise transgressive. Recognizing the limits of feminist transgression has helped me to analyze more carefully the politics of child rearing, which in turn has led me back to analyzing feminism. Individual parenting choices—teaching resistance to stereotypes, for example—clearly are political in origin and intent. Less clear, perhaps because less consciously chosen, is the larger political statement my family makes, which provides the framework for all other choices. Although Doug and I did not choose to have children for political reasons, having them and nurturing them was and *is* a political act, as Williams's remarks imply. And like all successful politics, this political act is rooted in love.

At about the same time that I read *The Alchemy of Race and Rights*, I received a letter from an old friend, a black woman who had recently moved and begun a new teaching job. "It is really an urban, poor area," she wrote. "We are overcrowded and understaffed. This will be a big change from the affluence I'm used to. . . . Part of me wants to run to a plush suburb; most of me wants to use my expertise for *my* people and for poor people in general." As I read this letter, I experienced a heightened version of the doubled consciousness that has become familiar to me since Sean was born ten years ago. I knew just who Joanna meant by "*my* people," and shared her desire to put energies and expertise to their use. At the same time, I realized that I was outside that group, that her people were not actually my people, at least not in the forms of "likeness" that observers like Judge Sorkow would recognize. This letter pushed me to consider who "my people" are. Growing up, I thought of "my people" as Irish people; in young adulthood, this category shifted to women, especially feminists. Mothering Sean and Ailis has revised this category for me to "black people," although I am not a black person.

If by "my people" one means "the people I love, the people with whom I identify, the people on whose behalf I work," then my children are first among "my people." Loving Sean and Ailis so personally and so intensely has led me to a broader and less personal love of black people generally, because Sean's and Ailis's lives will be shaped by the fortunes of black people as a group. African-American feminist theorist bell hooks says in *Talking Back*, in the context of a discussion of love and politics, that "love can be understood as a powerful force that challenges and resists domination."[48] Love, following this logic, can be the basis of a politics of resistance and liberation. In fact, I would argue that love *must* be the basis of this politic and of any antiracist theorizing about race, any feminist theorizing about gender.

Patricia Hill Collins notes the large numbers of black women thinkers who make the connection between love and politics; for example, June Jordan: "as I seek to evaluate the potentiality, the life-supportive commitment/possibilities of anyone or anything, the decisive question is, always, *where is the love?*"[49] This question shows us what is missing in the sisterhood model of feminism, despite its name, and also suggests what a comradeship model must be rooted in. I look at my daughter Ailis and see in her tiny face herself, the woman she will become, black women, and myself. Loving Ailis so profoundly leads me to love the black women with whom her lot is cast.

I love my children, and I have chosen to love blackness also, as I hope that Sean and Ailis will, in full awareness of the implications of that choice. In the opening chapter of *Black Looks* bell hooks says that "loving blackness" ought to be the basis of anti-racist, anti–white-supremacist politics. I think, as hooks also seems to, that the choice of loving blackness is open to whites as well as to blacks, and that it may be an empowering choice, allowing us to maintain independent, individual consciousnesses. Loving blackness is not the same thing as hating whiteness—just as feminism is not about hating men—and in fact the two are incompatible. Loving blackness requires more than a reactionary attention to blackness, whereas hating whiteness requires foregrounding whiteness. Loving blackness is about refusing to put whiteness at the center of everything, resisting white supremacist views of blackness, seeing the value of blackness. For me, a white person, loving blackness resembles Sara Ruddick's description of attentive love: a love that appreciates difference without desiring sameness, that loves the other person without trying to turn that person into a version of the self.[50]

White people cannot become black, but we can reject the privileges of whiteness, calling them what they are, and in that choice build a bridge across the color line, beginning the journey away from white essentialist attitudes that support racism and that undermine our humanity. Feminists should be in the vanguard of this bridge building. All of our lives depend on that bridge; without it we will surely drown.

Notes

Preface

1 Throughout this book I focus on blacks and whites, although I am well aware that many of the points I make about black people's lives in the United States could be made also about the lives of members of other "minority" groups. However, the particular stereotypes that could be applied to my son are not stereotypes of males in other groups.

2 Child development expert Bettye M. Caldwell, for instance, expressed this view in response to James P. Comer and Alvin F. Poussaint's *Raising Black Children* (New York: Plume, 1992). She told the *New York Times* that she has always worked against analyzing the differences between children in terms of race. See Carol Lawson, "Nurturing Black Children in an Unfriendly World," *New York Times*, 10 June 1993, C6.

3 Population figures come from the 1990 U.S. Census; family income from Andrew Hacker, *Two Nations* (New York: Scribners, 1992), 233; degree information from Hacker, *Two Nations*, 236.

4 The prison statistics come from Hacker, *Two Nations*, 197. The danger of arrest is so great for blacks, particularly young black males, that Comer and Poussaint devote a section of *Raising Black Children* to explaining what parents should do if their child is jailed (388–392). This material would never appear in a "color-blind"—that is, white-oriented—parenting manual. Victim and employment statistics from Hacker, *Two Nations*, 183 and 111 respectively.

5 Statistics from Hacker, *Two Nations*: unemployment, 103; poverty, 100; family earnings differential, 94.

6 Cornel West makes a similar point in *Race Matters* (Boston: Beacon Press, 1993), 1.

7 Ibid., 2–3. Emphasis in original.

One. On Lines and Bridges

1 Cherríe Moraga and Gloria Anzaldúa, editors of *This Bridge Called My Back: Writings by Radical Women of Color* (Watertown, Mass.:

Persephone Press, 1981), employ the bridge metaphor differently. Although I was familiar with this text at the time of my bridge panic, I did not see the racial analogy in my own life until years later.

2   W.E.B. DuBois, *The Souls of Black Folk* (1903; reprint, New York: Viking Penguin, 1989), 1.

3   Victoria Benning and Philip Bennett, "Racial lines shadow new generation," *Boston Globe*, 13 September 1992, 1, 30–31.

4   Victoria Benning and Philip Bennett, "Questions of race confound anew," *Boston Globe*, 14 September 1992, 6.

5   Benning and Bennett, "Racial lines," 31.

6   Kwame Anthony Appiah, "Race," in Frank Lentricchia and Thomas McLaughlin, eds., *Critical Terms for Literary Study* (Chicago: University of Chicago Press, 1990), 277.

7   Statistic from United States Bureau of the Census, *Current Population Reports*, Series P-20, No. 445.

8   See Kathy Russell, Midge Wilson, and Ronald Hall, *The Color Complex* (New York: Harcourt Brace Jovanovich, 1992), 116–118, for additional ways in which interracial marriages are stereotyped. After reading this section, a white friend expressed surprise about the current stereotype among progressive whites, noting that in the 1950s and 1960s interracial marriages were seen as highly positive by progressive whites. Remnants of this attitude—which is of course also racist—persist among some whites. On several occasions, whites who have never met Doug have remarked to me that they think our marriage is "cool" or "great." How would they know? What they're expressing is as much a stereotype as the more obviously negative ones discussed in the text.

9   This history can be read in numerous places, including Paula Giddings's *When and Where I Enter: The Impact of Black Women on Race and Sex in America* (New York: William Morrow, 1984).

10 Patricia Hill Collins, *Black Feminist Thought: Knowledge, Consciousness, and the Politics of Empowerment* (New York: Routledge, 1991), 50.

11 Derrick Bell, *And We Are Not Saved: The Elusive Quest for Racial Justice* (New York: Basic Books, 1987), 49.

12 Ibid., 207.

13 West, *Race Matters*, 12.

14 I deal more directly with black women's particular objections in chapter 6.

15 Derrick Bell's fictional cab driver in *Faces at the Bottom of the Well: The Permanence of Racism* (New York: Basic Books, 1992) details how those blacks who have "made it" unwittingly hurt other blacks (25–28).

16 While I was writing this book, Douglas Bates published his memoir about parenting across racial lines, *Gift Children: A Story of Race, Family, and Adoption in a Divided America* (New York: Ticknor and Fields, 1993), but as the title makes clear, his book is about adoption. Bates and his wife, both white, adopted two black girls. This situation is fundamentally different from my own.

Two. Starting Out

1 Richard Dyer, "White," *Screen* 29, no. 4 (Autumn 1988): 44.

2 Hettie Jones, *How I Became Hettie Jones* (New York: Dutton, 1990), 202.

3 Jane Lazarre, *Worlds Beyond My Control* (New York: Dutton, 1991), xiv.

4 Ibid., xiii–xiv.

5 Ralph Ellison, *Invisible Man* (1952; reprint, New York: Random House, 1972), 16.

6 Mark Mathabane and Gail Mathabane, *Love in Black and White* (New York: HarperCollins, 1992), 42.

7 Audre Lorde, *Sister Outsider* (Freedom, Calif.: The Crossing Press, 1984), 127.

8 Peggy McIntosh's "White Privilege and Male Privilege: A Personal Account of Coming to See Correspondences Through Work in Women's Studies," further details the privileges that attend whiteness in this society. In Margaret L. Andersen and Patricia Hill Collins, eds., *Race, Class, and Gender: An Anthology* (Belmont, Calif.: Wadsworth, 1992). I want to thank Martha Roth for pointing out the ways in which members of other "minority" groups are asked to speak for the entire group.

9 Bell, *Faces*, 172.

10 Ibid., 6.

11 Douglas Bates remarks on a similar lack of thought regarding his and his wife's decision to adopt. *Gift Children*, 29.

Three. "Why Do White People Have Vaginas?"

1   Reed's remarks are quoted by bell hooks in *Yearning: race, gender, and cultural politics* (Boston: South End Press, 1990), 74.

2   Henry Louis Gates, Jr., "Writing 'Race' and the Difference It Makes," *Critical Inquiry* 12 (Autumn 1985): 5.

3   Collins, *Black Feminist Thought*, 27.

4   Catherine and Sherry Bunin, *Is That Your Sister?* (New York: Pantheon, 1976); Adrienne Jones, *So, Nothing Is Forever* (Boston: Houghton Mifflin, 1974).

5   Manthia Diawara, "Black Spectatorship: Problems of Identification and Resistance," *Screen* 29, no. 4 (Autumn 1988): 66–67.

6   See, for instance, the studies cited by Letty Cottin Pogrebin in *Growing Up Free* (New York: McGraw-Hill, 1980) and Nancy Chodorow's work on cross-cultural studies of gender in *Feminism and Psychoanalytic Theory* (New Haven: Yale University Press, 1989).

7   Joanne M. Braxton, *Black Women Writing Autobiography: A Tradition Within a Tradition* (Philadelphia: Temple University Press, 1989), 3.

8   Collins, *Black Feminist Thought*, 124–128.

9   Aida Hurtado, "Relating to Privilege: Seduction and Rejection in the Subordination of White Women and Women of Color," *Signs* 14 (1989): 843–855, discusses the differences between stereotypes of white women and those of women of color.

10 See, for example, Haki R. Madhubuti, *Black Men: Obsolete, Single, Dangerous?* (Chicago: Third World Press, 1992), and Ed Wiley III, "Too Few Higher Education Initiatives Aim to Reverse Plight of Young Black Males, Say Education Experts," *Black Issues in Higher Education* 11 (March 1993): 18. Calvin Hernton warns about the dangers to *all* black people inherent in the "ideology of race first and sex second" in his article on Anita Hill, "Breaking Silences," in Robert Chrisman and Robert L. Allen, eds., *Court of Appeal* (New York: Ballantine Books, 1992), 86.

11 Jane Lazarre pointed out to me the popularity of the warrior identity among young black men. Private correspondence, August 26, 1993.

Four. "One Drop of Black Blood"

1 Russell, Wilson, and Hall note that it is very common for black children to see whiteness as desirable. *The Color Complex*, 63–64. I am grateful to Martha Roth for reminding me of what I had forgotten: that many white children look for some exotic ancestor to redeem them from ordinariness.

2 James Weldon Johnson, *The Autobiography of an Ex-Coloured Man* (1912; reprint, New York: Vintage, 1989), 16.

3 Ibid., 18.

4 Zora Neale Hurston, *Their Eyes Were Watching God* (1937; reprint, Urbana: University of Illinois Press, 1980), 21.

5 Ibid.

6 James P. Comer and Alvin F. Poussaint, *Black Child Care* (New York: Simon and Schuster, 1976), 17.

7 Collins, *Black Feminist Thought*, 69.

8 A story in the October 1990 *Ebony* by Kathleen Cross describes the problems inherent in "living Black and looking White"; titled "Trapped in the Body of a White Woman," this first-person story details the author's attempts to be "black enough," (70).

9 Diawara, "Black Spectatorship," 70–71.

10 bell hooks, *Black Looks: Race and Representation* (Boston: South End Press, 1992), 31–32.

11 Russell, Wilson, and Hall, *The Color Complex*, 18.

12 Frederick Douglass, *Narrative of the Life of Frederick Douglass*, in Henry Louis Gates, Jr., ed., *The Classic Slave Narratives* (New York: New American Library, 1987), 257.

13 W.E.B. DuBois, "In Black," and Marcus Garvey, "An Exposé of the Caste System Among Negroes," both in John Bracey, Jr., August Meier, and Elliot Rudwick, eds., *Black Nationalism in America* (New York: Bobbs Merrill, 1970), 276–278 and 201–209.

14 Collins, *Black Feminist Thought*, 78–82.

15 Ibid., 80.

16 Ibid., 79.

17 hooks, *Black Looks*, 3.

18 Alice Walker, "If the Present Looks Like the Past, Then What Does the Future Look Like?" in *In Search of Our Mothers' Gardens* (New York: Harcourt Brace Jovanovich, 1982), 291.

19 Ibid., 311.

20 Darlene Powell Hopson and Derek Hopson, *Different and Wonderful: Raising Black Children in a Race-Conscious Society* (New York: Prentice-Hall, 1990).

21 Russell, Wilson, and Hall, *The Color Complex*, 99.

22 Quotation from Alvin F. Poussaint, "Foreword" to Hopson and Hopson, *Different and Wonderful*, xiii.

23 Njeri's remarks are quoted in Lena Williams, "Blacks struggle with the question of what it means to be black," *Providence Sunday Journal*, 19 January 1992, D-2.

24 Quotation from Amiri Baraka, "The Legacy of Malcolm X, and the Coming of the Black Nation," in Abraham Chapman, ed., *New Black Voices* (New York: New American Library, 1972), 463.

25 Ibid., 464.

26 Steve Biko, *I Write What I Like* (San Francisco: Harper and Row, 1978), 48.

27 Toni Morrison, *Jazz* (New York: Knopf, 1992), 143.

28 N. S. Charles, "Black Soldiers in Somalia," *Emerge* (May 1993): 20.

29 This incident predated Oprah Winfrey's televised interview with Jackson, in which the singer revealed that he suffers from a medical problem that has lightened his skin. The medical condition does not explain Jackson's narrow nose, cleft chin, and other features, however.

30 Johnson, *Autobiography*, 210.

31 Ibid., 211.

32 Figures from Collins, *Black Feminist Thought*, 59.

33 Comer and Poussaint, *Raising Black Children*, 287.

34 Ibid., 303.

35 West, *Race Matters*, 26

36 Ibid., 28–29.

37 Molefi Kete Asante, "Racism, Consciousness, and Afrocentricity," in Gerald Early, ed., *Lure and Loathing* (New York: Penguin, 1993), 142.

38 Russell, Wilson, and Hall, *The Color Complex*, 76.

39 See ibid., 77–78, and Karen Grigsby Bates, "Color Complexity," *Emerge* (June 1993): 38–39.

Five. The Fourth R

1   Black use of this word is debated among blacks. For a good précis of the controversy see Darrell Dawsey, "Nigger," *Emerge* (June 1993): 35–36.

2   Collins, *Black Feminist Thought*, 85.

3   This strategy is widespread among black parents. See Lawson, "Nurturing Black Children," C-1, and Comer and Poussaint, *Raising*, 186–187.

4   Huey P. Newton, *Revolutionary Suicide* (New York: Harcourt Brace Jovanovich, 1973), 22.

5   Ibid., 23.

6   West, *Race Matters*, 3.

7   Bates, *Gift*, 117.

8   The key limitation here is *relied upon*. Many whites prove to be exceptions to this rule, and I am especially grateful to several white parents of white children who worked tirelessly with our parents' group.

9   hooks, *Black Looks*, 13.

10 See Marilyn Frye's "Oppression" for an examination of the implications of loosely using "oppression," in Paula S. Rothenberg, ed., *Race, Class, and Gender in the United States*, 2nd ed., (New York: St. Martin's, 1991), 54–57.

11 Comer and Poussaint, *Raising*, 240–241.

12 Hopson and Hopson, *Different and Wonderful*, 152.

13 Ibid., 42.

14 Bell, *Faces*, 113.

15 D. Bates, *Gift*, 118–119.

16 Russell, Wilson, and Hall, *The Color Complex*, 101.

17 Hopson and Hopson make a similar point, in *Different and Wonderful*, 141.

18 Hacker, *Two Nations*, 22.

19 Ibid., 22–23.

20 See Comer and Poussaint, *Raising*, 190–191.

21 An example of this dismissive attitude is a recent cover article by Heather MacDonald for *The New Republic*, "The Diversity Industry" (5 July 1993): 22–25, in which the author mocks efforts at cross-cultural communication.

22 Hacker, *Two Nations*, 29.

23 They are proved wrong by a recent study by Patricia G. Ramsey that suggests that even very young children do grasp the social ramifications

of racial differences. "The Salience of Race in Young Children Growing Up in an All-White Community," *Journal of Educational Psychology* 83 (1991): 31–33.

24   bell hooks, *Feminist Theory From Margin to Center* (Boston: South End Press, 1984), 54.

Six. Mothers, Daughters, Sisters, Comrades

1   I am ignoring the reactions of overtly racist whites here, as no connection with them seems to me either possible or even desirable.

2   Lorde, *Sister Outsider*, 43–44.

3   Nancie Caraway makes a similar point in *Segregated Sisterhood: Racism and the Politics of American Feminism* (Knoxville: University of Tennessee Press, 1991), 188–191, giving a series of examples.

4   These criticisms have also been made in public forums. For instance, in an edition of PBS's *Frontline* (1993) devoted to black community responses to Anita Hill's charges against Clarence Thomas, several black women identified themselves as feminist but roundly criticized white feminists for their lack of sensitivity to the specifically racial issues Hill's charges raised, a lack of sensitivity and understanding that the women interviewed apparently regarded as typical.

5   Maria C. Lugones discusses limitations of the sororal model in "Sisterhood and Friendship as Feminist Models," in Cheris Kramarae and Dale Spender, eds., *The Knowledge Explosion* (New York: Teachers College Press, 1992), 406–408.

6   Caraway also discusses the limitations of a sororal model for feminism. *Segregated Sisterhood*, 199–200.

7   Collins describes black women who act politically from the "othermother" position as "community othermothers." *Black Feminist Thought*, 129–130.

8   The notion of early "second wave" feminism as primarily a (white) daughter's critique was first suggested to me by Paula Bennett in a telephone discussion of feminist mothering in 1989.

9   bell hooks notes the life-style/politics divergence in a *Ms.* magazine round-table discussion, and says, "I want people to advocate feminism as a politics. Feminism is perceived as a lifestyle, as something you

become rather than something you *do.* I'm concerned about getting people to think of it as a movement to change something." "Let's Get Real About Feminism," *Ms.* 4, no. 2 (1993): 38.

10 See Gloria Joseph's chapters in Gloria Joseph and Jill Lewis, *Common Differences* (Garden City, N.Y.: Anchor, 1981), especially 95–105.

11 "Maternal Reading: Lazarre and Walker" in Brenda O. Daly and Maureen T. Reddy, eds., *Narrating Mothers: Theorizing Maternal Subjectivities* (Knoxville: University of Tennessee Press, 1991), 222–238.

12 Elizabeth Abel notes this tendency among white feminist critics who work on black women's writing. "Black Writing, White Reading: Race and the Politics of Feminist Interpretation," *Critical Inquiry* 19 (Spring 1993): 472–474.

13 In this chapter I am building in part on Elizabeth Schultz's "Out of the Woods and into the World: A Study of Interracial Friendships Between Women in American Novels," in Marjorie Pryse and Hortense J. Spillers, eds., *Conjuring: Black Women, Fiction, and Literary Tradition* (Bloomington: Indiana University Press, 1985), 67–85. In that article, Schultz sets white male authors' portrayals of interracial friendships against those invented by black women and men and by white women. She points out that most novels by black women that include such a relationship suggest that interracial friendships cannot endure through time (82).

14 Toni Morrison, *Beloved* (New York: Knopf, 1987), 79.

15 Ibid., 80.

16 Ibid., 84.

17 Sherley Anne Williams, *Dessa Rose* (New York: William Morrow, 1986), 83.

18 Ibid., 114, ellipses in original.

19 Alice Walker, *Meridian* (1976; New York: Pocket Books, 1986), 112.

20 Ibid., 107.

21 Ibid., 108.

22 Abel, "Black Writing, White Reading," 471, especially n. 2.

23 S. Williams, *Dessa*, 169.

24 Ibid., 158.

25 Walker, *Meridian*, 142.

26 Schultz points out the contrast in black and white women novelists' treatments of "sex's historical role in reinforcing the peculiar intensity of American racism": for the most part, white women novelists ignore

the sexual dimension of racism, while "in novels by black women the difficulties of a black and a white woman's achieving friendship are exacerbated by sexual competition and by the sexual dimension of American racism" (77–78).

27 Walker, *Meridian*, 149.

28 Ibid., 173–174.

29 Sara Ruddick, *Maternal Thinking: Toward a Politics of Peace* (Boston: Beacon Press, 1989).

30 Collins, *Black Feminist Thought*, 119–122.

31 Lorde, *Sister Outsider*, 74.

32 Walker, *Meridian*, 175, emphasis in original.

33 S. Williams, *Dessa*, 101.

34 Ibid., 102.

35 This argument is rooted in Nancy Chodorow's *The Reproduction of Mothering* (Berkeley: University of California Press, 1978).

36 S. Williams, *Dessa*, 93.

37 See Williams, ibid., 95–97, for examples.

38 Ibid., 128–129.

39 Ibid., 170.

40 Ibid., 201–202.

41 Ibid., 211.

42 Ibid., 212.

43 See Lugones, "Sisterhood and Friendship," 407.

44 See ibid., 407 and 410.

45 See Gloria Joseph's chapters in *Common Differences* and chapter 6 in Collins, *Black Feminist Thought*.

46 Patricia J. Williams, *The Alchemy of Race and Rights* (Cambridge: Harvard University Press, 1991), 226–227.

47 Lasana Cazembe, "Transracial adoption is a ploy," in "From the Readers," *Colors* 2, no. 5 (September–October 1993): 8.

48 hooks, *Talking*, 26.

49 Collins, *Black Feminist Thought*, 197.

50 I am grateful to Brenda Daly, Sara Ruddick, and Jean Fagan Yellin, who read earlier drafts of this chapter and gave me helpful criticisms.

Bibliography

Abel, Elizabeth. "Black Writing, White Reading: Race and the Politics of Feminist Interpretation." *Critical Inquiry* 19 (Spring 1993): 470–498.

Appiah, Kwame Anthony. "Race." In *Critical Terms for Literary Study*, edited by Frank Lentricchia and Thomas McLaughlin. 274–287. Chicago: University of Chicago Press, 1990.

Asante, Kete Molefi. "Racism, Consciousness, and Afrocentricity." In *Lure and Loathing*, edited by Gerald Early. 127–143. New York: Penguin, 1993.

Baraka, Amiri. "The Legacy of Malcolm X, and the Coming of the Black Nation." In *New Black Voices*, edited by Abraham Chapman. 458–467. New York: New American Library, 1972.

Bates, Douglas. *Gift Children: A Story of Race, Family, and Adoption in a Divided America*. New York: Ticknor and Fields, 1993.

Bates, Karen Grigsby. "Color Complexity." *Emerge* (June 1993): 38–39.

Bell, Derrick. *And We Are Not Saved: The Elusive Quest for Racial Justice*. New York: Basic Books, 1987.

———. *Faces at the Bottom of the Well: The Permanence of Racism*. New York: Basic Books, 1992.

Benning, Victoria, and Philip Bennett. "Questions of race confound anew." *Boston Globe*, 14 September 1992, p. 1.

———. "Racial lines shadow new generation." *Boston Globe*, 13 September 1992, p. 1.

Biko, Steve. *I Write What I Like*. San Francisco: Harper and Row, 1978.

Bradley, David. *The Chaneysville Incident*. New York: Harper and Row, 1981.

Braxton, Joanne M. *Black Women Writing Autobiography: A Tradition Within a Tradition*. Philadelphia: Temple University Press, 1989.

Bunin, Catherine, and Sherry Bunin. *Is That Your Sister?* New York: Pantheon, 1976.

Butler, Octavia. *Kindred*. 1979. Reprint. Boston: Beacon Press, 1988.

Caraway, Nancie. *Segregated Sisterhood: Racism and the Politics of American Feminism*. Knoxville: University of Tennessee Press, 1991.

Cazembe, Lasana. "Transracial adoption is a ploy." Letter in "From the Readers." *Colors* 2, no. 5 (September–October 1993): 7–8.

Charles, N. S. "Black Soldiers in Somalia: Mixed Emotions, Vanishing Euphoria." *Emerge* (May 1993): 19–20.

Chodorow, Nancy. *Feminism and Psychoanalytic Theory*. New Haven: Yale University Press, 1989.

———. *The Reproduction of Mothering*. Berkeley: University of California Press, 1978.

Collins, Patricia Hill. *Black Feminist Thought: Knowledge, Consciousness, and the Politics of Empowerment*. New York: Routledge, 1991.

Comer, James P., and Alvin F. Poussaint. *Black Child Care*. New York: Simon and Schuster, 1976.

———. *Raising Black Children*. New York: Plume, 1992.

Cross, Kathleen. "Trapped in the Body of a White Woman." *Ebony* (October 1990): 70–74.

Dawsey, Darrell. "Nigger." *Emerge* (June 1993): 35–36.

Diawara, Manthia. "Black Spectatorship: Problems of Identification and Resistance." *Screen* 29, no. 4 (1988): 66–76.

Douglass, Frederick. *Narrative of the Life of Frederick Douglass*. In *The Classic Slave Narratives*, edited by Henry Louis Gates, Jr. 243–331. New York: New American Library, 1987.

DuBois, W.E.B. "In Black." In *Black Nationalism in America*, edited by John Bracey, Jr., August Meier, and Elliot Rudwick. 276–278. New York: Bobbs Merrill, 1970.

———. *The Souls of Black Folk*. 1903. Reprint. New York: Penguin, 1989.

Dyer, Richard. "White." *Screen* 29, no. 4 (1988): 44–64.

Ellison, Ralph. *Invisible Man*. 1952. Reprint. New York: Random House, 1972.

Faludi, Susan. *Backlash: The Undeclared War Against American Women*. New York: Crown, 1991.

Frye, Marilyn. "Oppression." In *Race, Class, and Gender in the United States*, edited by Paula S. Rothenberg. 54–57. New York: St. Martin's, 1991.

Garland, Sarah. *Billy and Belle*. New York: Viking, 1992.

Garvey, Marcus. "An Exposé of the Caste System Among Negroes." In *Black Nationalism in America*, edited by John Bracey, Jr., August Meier, and Elliot Rudwick. 207–209. New York: Bobbs Merrill, 1970.

Gates, Henry Louis, Jr. "Writing 'Race' and the Difference It Makes." *Critical Inquiry* 12 (1985): 1–20.

Giddings, Paula. *When and Where I Enter: The Impact of Black Women on Race and Sex in America*. New York: William Morrow, 1984.

Hacker, Andrew. *Two Nations*. New York: Scribners, 1992.

Havill, Juanita. *Jamaica's Find*. Boston: Houghton Mifflin, 1986.

Hernton, Calvin. "Breaking Silences." *Court of Appeal*, edited by Robert Chrisman and Robert L. Allen. 86–91. New York: Ballantine Books, 1992.

hooks, bell. *Black Looks: Race and Representation*. Boston: South End Press, 1992.

———. *Feminist Theory From Margin to Center*. Boston: South End Press, 1984.

———. *Talking Back: Thinking Feminist, Thinking Black*. Boston: South End Press, 1989.

———. *Yearning: race, gender, and cultural politics*. Boston: South End Press, 1990.

hooks, bell, Gloria Steinem, Urvashi Vaid, and Naomi Wolf. "Let's Get Real about Feminism." *Ms.* 4, no. 2 (1993): 34–43.

Hopson, Darlene Powell, and Derek Hopson. *Different and Wonderful: Raising Black Children in a Race-Conscious Society*. New York: Prentice-Hall, 1990.

Hurston, Zora Neale. *Their Eyes Were Watching God*. 1937. Reprint. Urbana: University of Illinois Press, 1980.

Hurtado, Aida. "Relating to Privilege: Seduction and Rejection in the Subordination of White Women and Women of Color." *Signs* 14 (1989): 843–855.

Johnson, James Weldon. *The Autobiography of An Ex-Coloured Man*. 1912. Reprint. New York: Vintage, 1989.

Jones, Adrienne. *So, Nothing is Forever*. Boston: Houghton Mifflin, 1974.

Jones, Hettie. *How I Became Hettie Jones*. New York: Dutton, 1990.

Joseph, Gloria, and Jill Lewis. *Common Differences*. Garden City, N.Y.: Anchor, 1981.

Kozol, Jonathan. *Savage Inequalities: Children in America's Schools*. New York: Crown, 1991.

Lawson, Carol. "Nurturing Black Children in an Unfriendly World." *New York Times*, 10 June 1993. C1.

Lazarre, Jane. *The Mother Knot*. 1976. Reprint. Boston: Beacon Press, 1986.

———. *Worlds Beyond My Control*. New York: Dutton, 1991.

Lorde, Audre. *Sister Outsider*. Freedom, Calif.: The Crossing Press, 1984.

Lugones, Maria C. "Sisterhood and Friendship as Feminist Models." In *The Knowledge Explosion*, edited by Cheris Kramarae and Dale Spender. 406–412. New York: Teachers College Press, 1992.

MacDonald, Heather. "The Diversity Industry." *The New Republic* (5 July 1993) 22–25.

Madhubuti, Haki R. *Black Men: Obsolete, Single, Dangerous?* Chicago: Third World Press, 1992.

Mathabane, Mark, and Gail Mathabane. *Love in Black and White.* New York: HarperCollins, 1992.

McIntosh, Peggy. "White Privilege and Male Privilege: A Personal Account of Coming to See Correspondences Through Work in Women's Studies." In *Race, Class, and Gender: An Anthology*, edited by Margaret L. Andersen and Patricia Hill Collins. 70–81. Belmont, Calif.: Wadsworth, 1992.

Moraga, Cherríe, and Gloria Anzaldúa, eds. *This Bridge Called My Back: Writings By Radical Women of Color.* Watertown, Mass.: Persephone Press, 1981.

Morrison, Toni. *Beloved.* New York: Knopf, 1987.

———. *Jazz.* New York: Knopf, 1992.

Newton, Huey P. *Revolutionary Suicide.* New York: Harcourt Brace Jovanovich, 1973.

Pogrebin, Letty Cottin. *Growing Up Free.* New York: McGraw-Hill, 1980.

Poussaint, Alvin F. "Foreword." xiii–xvi. In Darlene Powell Hopson and Derek Hopson, *Different and Wonderful: Raising Black Children in a Race-Conscious Society.* New York: Prentice-Hall, 1990.

Ramsey, Patricia G. "The Salience of Race in Young Children Growing Up in an All-White Community." *Journal of Educational Psychology* 83 (1991): 28–34.

Reddy, Maureen T. "Maternal Reading: Lazarre and Walker." In *Narrating Mothers: Theorizing Maternal Subjectivities*, edited by Brenda O. Daly and Maureen T. Reddy. 222–238. Knoxville: University of Tennessee Press, 1991.

Ruddick, Sara. *Maternal Thinking: Toward a Politics of Peace.* Boston: Beacon Press, 1989.

Russell, Kathy, Midge Wilson, and Ronald Hall. *The Color Complex.* New York: Harcourt Brace Jovanovich, 1992.

Schultz, Elizabeth. "Out of the Woods and into the World: A Study of Interracial Friendships Between Women in American Novels." In *Conjuring: Black Women, Fiction, and Literary Tradition*, edited by Marjorie Pryse and Hortense J. Spillers. 67–85. Bloomington: Indiana University Press, 1985.

Walker, Alice. *In Search of Our Mothers' Gardens*. New York: Harcourt Brace Jovanovich, 1982.

————. *Meridian*. 1976. Reprint. New York: Pocket Books, 1986.

West, Cornel. *Race Matters*. Boston: Beacon Press, 1993.

Wiley, Ed, III. "Too Few Higher Education Initiatives Aim to Reverse Plight of Young Black Males, Say Education Experts." *Black Issues in Higher Education* (11 March 1993): 18.

Williams, Lena. "Blacks struggle with question of what it means to be black." *Providence Sunday Journal*, 19 January 1992, D-1.

Williams, Patricia J. *The Alchemy of Race and Rights*. Cambridge: Harvard University Press, 1991.

Williams, Sherley Anne. *Dessa Rose*. New York: William Morrow, 1986.

Index

About the Author

Maureen Reddy is an associate professor of English and director of the Women's Studies Program at Rhode Island College. She did her undergraduate work at Boston College and received her Ph.D. from the University of Minnesota. Her previous books include *Sisters in Crime: Feminism and the Crime Novel* and *Narrating Mothers: Theorizing Maternal Subjectivities* (with Brenda Daly). The daughter of Irish immigrants, Reddy has been part of a multiracial family for nearly two decades. *Crossing the Color Line* joins her academic fields with her personal experience in its focus on race and mothering. Reddy lives in Rhode Island with her husband, their two children, and various pets.